BECOMING

Forever

FAMILIES

BECOMING Forever FAMILIES

ROBERT CALLAWAY

atmosphere press

Note: This book is a sequel to the books *Through the Eyes of Asperger's: A Latter-day Saint Perspective* and *Living a Miracle* by Robert Callaway. In order to understand the continuity of the story presented here, it is recommended that the previous books be read, especially *Living a Miracle*. This sequel continues the story of the Wilkinson family, along with Ruth's story, and shows all of us how our Savior will lovingly help us to become forever families as we sincerely strive to follow Him. It shows the great blessings our Savior has for us, including true happiness, as we positively endure our trials and accept the wonderful, kind assistance which Christ especially desires to give us throughout our lives here on Earth.

This story contained herein is fictionalized, but is realistic in its approach as it demonstrates real-life experiences with some emotional episodes. It includes a few elements from *Through the Eyes of Asperger's: A Latter-day Saint Perspective* and *Living a Miracle*. Any similarity of names in this story to actual people and families is purely coincidental.

Table of Contents

Our Eternal Journey

THE MIRACLE OF MORTALITY

ALONG with my books, *Through the Eyes of Asperger's: A Latter-day Saint Perspective* and *Living a Miracle*, I, Robert Callaway, wrote this book about an extremely important subject: The actual process to follow that illustrates how our loving families are really able to continue living together forever. This is something that everyone desires, as we already have very strong emotional connections with our family members. We really don't want our families to end with the phrase, "Till death do us part."

Our loving Savior has a greater plan for us, because there is no sense for us to be born into families on this Earth, only to have it all end when we die. The plan for us to be members of families now is only the beginning of a magnificent plan, where we will be able to perform many greater acts of service as families, which will bring eternal blessings, including family increase. There is much waiting for us in our futures, especially after this life, as we choose to do a few simple things, items which our Lord knows will enable us to continue living with our loving families forever. These items are eloquently illustrated in this story which I will present here, and you will see how they are very easily accomplished by living through our trials.

This Earth life for us, this "Miracle of Mortality" is so very important for each of us to complete. This life is truly a miracle, because by successfully completing this life of learning through trial and error, we will be able to progress even more toward the ultimate blessing available to all of us, that of living with our loving Heavenly Father again in great love with our families forever, and experiencing true eternal joy, which will be full as our families continue to increase, and as we bring great joy to other people's lives forever. This is such a wonderful, glorious goal to look toward, as we do our best to live our lives in accordance with the teachings and guidance our loving Savior has given us and is giving us. We refer to Him as our Savior, being that He has accomplished His atoning sacrifice so that we have the wonderful opportunity to be "saved" as forever families, with majestic blessings which will continue forever, and so that we will not just continue on only as single individuals after this life, forfeiting all these blessings and inheritances which are lovingly offered to us. Reason demands that family relationships will continue after death.

Our present life is called "mortality" because our Lord intends our imperfect, frail bodies to die, so that we can continue progressing according to His perfect plan. Without death in this existence, our progression would be stopped, thus voiding our Savior's atoning sacrifice. However, after death, *everyone* will be resurrected in some future time, to a perfect body which is not able to physically die, thus we will become immortal. The degree of glorification our immortal bodies will receive depends on our actions and our faithfulness in this life now. One of these degrees of glorification includes our families living together forever.

We shouldn't think that because we are not perfect, as we continue to make mistakes, that we are never able to become like Christ and receive His great blessings. We don't have to be perfect in this life to be saved. If this were required, no one would be saved, except for Jesus Christ. This is obviously not His plan. His atoning sacrifice enables us to become perfect later, as we do our best now; and through sincere, daily repentance, with our intents and our hearts set on following Christ, while we progress by pressing forward on our covenant path leading to Him, we *will* receive all the blessings our Savior has for us, including living with our families forever.

Now is the day of our salvation, so if we're working zealously in this life—though we haven't fully overcome the world and we haven't done all we hoped we might do—we're still going to be saved and receive these blessings. We don't have to have an excessive zeal that becomes fanatical and unbalancing. We just need to live an upright life, follow Christ, and keep His commandments. We should work on loving Him as little children do, and loving to become like Him, following Him each day, and developing His love within us as we help other people. Even if we are far from being like Christ, if we are doing our best to live as He desires us to live, with sincere intent in our hearts to follow Him, He will give us the blessings we sincerely desire.

Those who have not received as much of Christ's law in this life will still be eligible to receive all of His blessings He has for each of us, as they live upright lives and desire and strive to follow Christ as much as they are able.

This story will show us how this reality is easily accomplished throughout our challenges in life, and how true repentance will allow us to return to our covenant path toward Christ, and how we will be able to receive all of our Savior's blessings, even after committing serious sins. It will show how we can easily develop faith and trust in Christ, and have more hope in the future as we live through our trials in life.

I, Robert Callaway, will begin this great presentation about becoming forever families by giving some wonderful, inspiring information concerning the importance of families in this life, as well as our Lord's plan for our families in the future. Then, throughout this story, I will show what exciting achievements and blessings are possible in our lives now as we place our faith and trust in Christ throughout our difficulties. I will show how He will help us in our righteous endeavors. Let's begin now with an introductory explanation concerning the power of our families, from our Lord's perspective.

Chapter One
THE POWER OF FAMILY

Ethan's story from my books, *Through the Eyes of Asperger's: A Latter-day Saint Perspective* and *Living a Miracle* shows what a person with Asperger's Syndrome is able to accomplish and what he is able to do for his family. These accounts also show the role that each family member has in the process. Sarah and Alexis helped Ethan with his trials through their support and love. Through their prayers and their words of encouragement, he was able to significantly progress. They also progressed by having this experience with Ethan and Asperger's Syndrome. This all occurred from the natural strong family connection and the power of love involved among the family members. Even though there are trials, struggles, challenges, and even disabilities involved, by everyone working together with love, the Lord's plans will be accomplished, and everyone involved can, and will progress, as would be the case in any family. People will learn to be more Christlike, and learn to have even more love toward each other as they continue on their journeys.

Departed family members in the Spirit World will be

helping us by watching over us with great love, by guiding us with thoughts and love we can feel from them, as they are very interested in our success and our progression toward our Savior. They will also be helping others understand the gospel. We will be helping them by performing ordinance work for our ancestors in the Lord's house, including sealings which will be connecting all of our family members together in love, as part of God's eternal family. We will also be helping them by remembering them in love and by doing our best. This is all done because we are showing true Christlike love toward each member of our family here on Earth and in the Spirit World, which is also right here. Remember, this is just the beginning of our grand eternal family filled with eternal love. This is our Savior's plan for us as families. By doing these things and by sincerely following Christ, all of our family members will be much closer to becoming an eternal family in the presence of God, united in great love. This is the whole purpose of our existence. Ethan's experience and that of his family, as previously related, shows how all this actually happens. This shows the power of family. Our Savior wants us to be truly happy now, and He wants us to be able to have true eternal joy along with greater blessings as families together, after this life. Being united and sealed as a family forever is the greatest of God's blessings for His children, allowing the opportunity to become as He is.

During this life here on Earth, it is extremely important that we follow the Lord's teachings and protect our families from Satan's deceptions. More than anything, Satan desires to tear families apart, as he knows the extreme importance and the wonderful magnificence of families in our Savior's eyes. A united family by God's law is the only way progression can occur in the eternities. This explains a little more about the power and significance of each family here on Earth.

Of course, no one is able to be perfect in this life, and through Satan's influence, at times family members will have quarrels, disagreements, and negative moods, and make wrong choices, which our Savior knows is necessary for us to experience, in order to grow and learn. Satan is allowed to influence people here on Earth, so we can learn and choose for ourselves to follow Christ as we learn the difference between right and wrong. We, individually and as families, will progress in the best possible manner as we choose to live by the teachings of our Savior in this type of setting. As it is so very important to Him that we do this, He has given us strong feelings of emotional connections and loving bonds with other members of our families. We want to help each other and have a continuing loving association with our family members. As we live Christ's gospel within our families, this loving bond will continue to increase, consistent with His plan for us.

Our Savior's loving plan for us as families is even greater during the millennium, our life here after His coming in glory. We, as families, and others will be involved in completing a greater amount of ordinance work in His temples, so that every person who has lived on this Earth, who is accountable and is capable of eternal progression, after having had the opportunity to hear and accept Christ's complete gospel, will be able to accept these ordinances in accordance with His law, in order to continue progressing. Those born into families during the millennium will also have this great opportunity. The righteous spirits of those who die before the age of accountability will automatically receive the blessings of being part of an eternal family, but will still need to be sealed to the family, if not born within the everlasting covenant of marriage according to God's law. This blessing is made possible by Christ's atoning sacrifice, which also provides this wonderful opportunity to continue progressing, with eternal increase as family units.

The culminating ordinance performed in the Lord's house involves the sealing of families together forever. This is the everlasting covenant of marriage. Our strong, loving family bonds will be increased, and we will feel even more of our Savior's pure love within us. This great feeling of Christlike love will be our dominant factor as we continue our wonderful progression as families. Those who are not sealed within families, after having chosen not to be, will not be progressing anymore, nor will they have any family increase at all. This shows the extreme importance of being sealed together as families. Our family life now is to show us the Lord's plan for us as we live each day within our families, so that we can understand more of His plan for our families later, and so that we can develop more love and the desire to serve others, beginning within our own families.

This is beautifully illustrated within the story in this sequel, where love is continuing to be shown within families, toward their loving family members with whom they have a loving bond; where people feel the great, compelling need to be included within a family, with the intense desire for this to continue forever. We all need to be recognized by others as individuals of worth, where we are wanted and needed and loved, and where we feel that we can contribute to other people's happiness and feel that we belong. This is a basic, innate need of every person on this Earth, placed within us by our loving Savior, so that, as mentioned, we can learn and have this continuing involvement with helping our family members and others, and showing Christlike love toward them for eternity.

I, Robert, will show how this beautiful concept plays out by continuing the story of Sarah, Ethan, and Alexis Wilkinson, beginning at the point where Ethan is serving his Church mission, and Alexis is away at college. I will show the wonderful blessings which will come into their lives, and into Ruth's life, as they all attempt to follow Christ during their lives each day throughout their trials, as they help and serve each other, and as they desire and work on doing what they need to do, in order to have their families continue forever.

Chapter Two

SARAH'S CONTINUING JOURNEY

SARAH has been very faithful during her trials in life with her family. She has been greatly blessed as she has put her faith and trust in Christ and sought God in prayer to give thanks for her blessings and to ask for needed comfort and assistance. Her two children are doing very well, as Ethan is progressing on his mission in the Church, and Alexis is doing excellent work at a fine restaurant as one of their main chefs, and is learning her class material very well in her studies at the State University in her major of culinary arts.

Recently, Sarah met a new member of her Church ward at church one Sunday. This person, Wayne Spencer, is close to her age, has been divorced, and has never had any children. Sarah is very excited after meeting him, and they both enjoy meeting with each other often to get to know each other better, and they enjoy going on outings together.

On a particular Sunday, after their church meetings have finished, Sarah invites Wayne to have dinner with her at her house. He graciously accepts and is excited that Sarah is showing more interest in him. Sarah is making one of her best three-course dinners for them. She is also very excited to share this time together. He comes to her house right on time and Sarah invites him inside.

She excitedly exclaims, "Wayne, it's so wonderful you could come and have dinner with me! It's so fun being with you!"

He responds, "I agree. Thank you so much for inviting me. We'll have a great evening together. I've really enjoyed getting to know you more these past few weeks. From what you've told me, your two children are doing wonderful."

"Yes, they are a great blessing to me."

Sarah goes into the kitchen where the food is ready to be served. Wayne helps her bring everything to the table, then he seats Sarah in her chair. After having a seat, she asks him to give a blessing on their dinner. He proceeds to say a great prayer and blessing, not only for their food, but for Sarah as well. Afterward, her face shows some emotion, which Wayne immediately notices.

He gently says, "Sarah, I feel even more now that you're a very, very spiritual person. I feel even closer to you. What are your thoughts?"

As they begin eating, she emotionally responds, "Wayne, I feel that you're a very spiritual person as well. I'm feeling that the Lord brought us together for a reason. I'm so happy that you started coming to church here in my ward."

"Yes, I felt this prompting that I should move into your ward, as I have been rather lonely in my previous ward. As you know, I was married for several years without having any children, and then my wife divorced me, which left me feeling devastated, like I'm not good enough for anyone." His face starts showing some sad emotion while saying this.

"I know somewhat how you feel. You remember I told you how I had a difficult time with this myself. But Christ has especially blessed me through all this. It's wonderful that you had the prompting that you should move into my ward and that we were able to meet. As we have been going out together and becoming more acquainted, I'm feeling closer to you, too. I feel your great spirituality when I look into your face. Do you feel that the Lord has more plans for us?"

Wayne suddenly experiences a very inspiring thought. Trying to get the words out, he emotionally says, with a trembling voice, "Sarah, I feel that the Lord has brought us together, and that He wants us to be sealed together as a family."

Sarah immediately puts her head down and sheds some tears. Wayne gets up and goes over to her, and puts his arm around her. After a moment, she looks up at him with a wet face, and very emotionally says, "Wayne, the Lord's Spirit has just confirmed this to me, that we should be married in the temple. We should both include this in our personal prayers tonight, and I feel it should happen soon, when we're both ready."

"I agree. Oh, this is such a wonderful evening we're having. For the past week, I haven't been able to stop thinking about you, and I was so excited when you invited me here tonight. It will be so fun making all our plans together. I'm so happy."

They joyfully finish their elegant dinner together while beginning the process of making plans for their wedding. They talk about Ethan's success on his Church mission in Argentina, and how he will be returning home in two months. Accordingly, they plan their wedding to be when he is home. Wayne plans to be at Sarah's house when Ethan calls to talk to his mom; they will then give him the exciting news. They also plan the time to tell Alexis at the State University, where she is more than halfway finished in completing her bachelor's degree.

As Wayne is still living in his apartment, they both agree that when they are married, he will give his notice to terminate his rental agreement and move in with Sarah. They are very excited thinking about these plans for the not-too-distant future.

After finishing their dinner, Wayne offers to help Sarah clear the table and clean up in the kitchen, which she graciously accepts. He then gives her a sincere compliment on her delicious food she prepared for them.

On hearing Wayne's compliment on her cooking, she responds, "Thank you so much! I try to prepare delicious meals, but you should taste Lexi's cooking. My daughter is studying culinary arts in college, and she prepared such delicious food when she was living here at home, even when she was barely a teenager. It was like eating at a fancy restaurant. She has loved cooking all her life, and I need to admit that the quality of her food surpasses mine. When Ethan comes home from his mission, we can plan a time for Lexi to prepare a great dinner for all of us, and you'll see what I mean."

"Oh, Sarah, that will be wonderful. I'm already looking forward to that time. It's so great that you have such talented children! You've told me how Ethan has overcome much of his Asperger's Syndrome and is so successful on his mission. I can't wait to meet both of them. They complete your family so well."

"Thank you, Wayne, for your compliment, but there is one other daughter I haven't told you about yet."

"Oh, there is? Who is she?"

Sarah lowers her head a little and begins to shed a few tears. She then looks up at Wayne, with her tender face showing great emotion. Seeing this, Wayne becomes a bit concerned and gently asks, "Sarah, what happened? Are you okay?"

"Yes, Wayne, I'm fine. It's just that I become emotional when I think about Trish. She was such a great member of the family, and she still is." Sarah sheds a couple more tears and continues with a trembling voice. "She passed on a few years ago when she was about eleven, from a severe tumor in her brain." Sarah pauses and lets out a few sobs. Wayne very tenderly puts his hand on her shoulder. "Trish was such a loving person, who taught us so much about Christlike love through her great example. She was a very tender, loving person. She's often in my thoughts. Here, I need to show you something very special."

They both go into the living room, to the wall where Trisha's painting is located. Wayne mentions, "Yes, I remember noticing this when I first came into your house. I thought that it is a great piece of art that you obtained, and didn't think more of it."

"Wayne, this is the painting I love, which Trish painted when she was only ten. She was a very talented artist."

"She painted that when she was ten? Sarah, it is simply beautiful! Looking at it more closely, it reminds me of the area where my family and I went camping when I was a young boy. It was a beautiful morning when the sun was coming up, shining through the trees, and a wonderful scent was in the mountain air. All the birds were chirping, and Mom and Dad were cooking pancakes and bacon on the grill. I'll always remember the special time we had then. It brings back such good memories."

"I'm so happy it brings good memories for you, too. This picture here is Trish, also when she was ten. This plaque underneath her painting was given to her at a surprise school assembly we all attended, which I'll always remember. It was so special."

"Sarah, she truly looks like an angel, with that angelic face of hers. I love her beautiful smile and her lovely hair. I can see how you miss her so much. That plaque must also have special meaning to you. I love the saying on it, 'To Trisha. You are a sweet, kind, loving, angelic person.' I would have loved to have known her while she was still here."

"Wayne, you know that when we are married in the temple, all three children will be yours, too, and after this life you will have the blessing to see her grow up from the age of her passing, and associate with her, and witness her perfect love." Sarah becomes very emotional, as she is touched with the

Spirit while saying this. "It will be such a blessing."

Wayne then becomes quite emotional himself, and solemnly says, "I haven't dreamed this could ever be possible for me, after having the life I've had. I definitely know the Lord has His plan to bless me now, because I felt that I should never give up. I'm so thankful the Lord heard my prayers and guided me to you. I've never felt so emotional before. I feel the Spirit telling me again that this is what we should do."

"I feel the Spirit here as well, and I wholeheartedly agree." They embrace each other tightly, and Wayne gives her a gentle kiss.

They sit down on the couch there, and talk a while longer about each other and about their immediate plans. They're so excited about this wonderful evening they've had for this pre-proposal, and both of them are very grateful for the Lord's blessings He is showing them at this time in their lives.

A few days later, Wayne asks Sarah out on a date, where they go have a special dinner together; he then brings her to his place, where he tells her he has a surprise for her. She is excited, not sure what he has in mind. After telling her what a great evening they've had so far, including a wonderful dinner and conversation, he has her sit on his couch, explaining that he has something else to tell her.

He grabs a small object from his pocket, kneels on one knee, opens the ring box he is holding, and asks with emotion, "Sarah, will you please marry me?"

Her eyes fill with tears and she embraces him very tightly, while mumbling a gentle, "Yes, I will."

Wayne also experiences a strong spiritual feeling during this precious time together, and thoughtfully responds with, "Thank you, Sarah. You mean so much to me." He gently slides the beautiful, sparkling ring on her finger, then hugs and kisses her. They spend a little more time sharing special moments together, and planning the date of their wedding, now that they are officially engaged.

The following Sunday afternoon, after attending some spiritual church meetings where many members congratulated Sarah and Wayne on their engagement, she invites him to her house, indicating that Ethan will be calling soon. Wayne is very excited to be able to talk to him. They joyfully chat with each other while waiting.

In under an hour, Sarah's phone rings, showing that Ethan is calling. She puts it on speaker, and answers, "Hello, Ethan?"

"Hi, Mom," he says with excitement. "How are you? You won't believe what happened today. An entire family, including their five children who are teenagers and one who is eleven, whom we have been teaching for a few weeks, felt the Lord's Spirit very strongly when we told them they can be a forever family after this life. They said that this is what they truly want, and are so very happy for the messages we have been giving them. They know this is the truth they've been waiting for all their lives. I can personally see the joy on each of their faces. We've now planned the date with them to join the Church. Isn't that wonderful?"

"Yes, Ethan, I'm so happy for you. I'm happy that you've progressed so well and that you are bringing true happiness to other people who are waiting for it."

"Thanks, Mom. I remember what grandfather told me at Trish's funeral, that I will be bringing happiness to other people. I didn't understand it at the time, but I felt he knew what he was saying. By the way, how's he doing now?"

"Oh, he's doing okay. He's a bit weaker and a little more tired, but his younger brother, your great uncle Richard, is taking good care of him at his house."

"That's good to hear. How's Lexi doing with her studies?"

"She's doing very well. She's in her third year to completing her bachelor's, and is planning to do some graduate work to further her culinary arts degree. She's already a great chef at a prestigious restaurant near the university, and is really enjoying it. How are you doing with your missionary companion?"

"Oh, Mom, I'm so glad you asked about that. Guess what? Three days ago, I was assigned a new companion to work with, and you won't believe this, but he has Asperger's Syndrome! My mission president told me that he's just beginning his mission here in Argentina, and that he needs someone who understands him better, to help him become adjusted to this new way of life. I'm assigned as his senior companion, and I've already been able to help him feel more comfortable around the people here, around the other missionaries, and with learning Spanish better. Thanks to the Lord and to Robert, I'm very comfortable teaching him and helping him. Isn't that wonderful?"

"Ethan, that's so good to hear! You've progressed so well. You can literally see how our Savior is blessing you. Now, I have some wonderful news to share with you. Are you ready? You know I've been telling you at times about this person I've met at church, and how we've been getting to know each other. Well, guess what? The Spirit has been prompting each of us about our futures, and the Spirit of the Lord prompted this person, named Wayne Spencer, to propose to me, which he did a couple of days ago. Ethan, I'm now engaged to be married to him in the temple. Isn't that wonderful?"

"Oh, Mom, it sure is. As you were just saying this, I felt the Lord's Spirit confirming this to me, and I now feel it so strongly." Ethan chokes up a bit as he continues. "Mom, remember that blessing I gave you soon after grandfather ordained me an Elder? The Lord promised then that you will receive a faithful husband and be married in the temple. We all see that our Savior certainly keeps His promises. This is so great to hear. Is he there with you?"

"Yes, I'm here. This is Wayne, and I'm so happy to hear you, to know more about you, and to feel of your spirituality. I'm very, very happy to be able to have a son like you. I haven't had any children of my own before, and I especially look forward to meeting you in person when you come home. This will be very exciting for me."

"It will be exciting for me to meet you, too. It's so great to have a forever dad now."

Sarah emotionally responds with great feeling. "It's so wonderful how the Lord is able to bless us. I certainly feel the presence of Trish here, and I feel she is also so very happy for all of us and for our temple marriage, which we have set to occur the third week after you're home from your mission. Lexi will also have a semester break at that time, so she will be able to be here with us also."

"That sounds so wonderful; I can hardly wait. I'm certainly enjoying my last weeks here on my mission so much that I wish I could stay here forever with these great people, but I know I need to do more things in my life when I return, and I'm so excited about having a great dad in my life. I can tell that Wayne is a wonderful person, and I guess that I should call him 'Dad' now, instead of 'Wayne.' Dad, are you listening?"

"Ethan, that's such a wonderful thing to hear for the first time in my life. It's so great to talk to you and be able to call you my son."

"Thanks, Dad. It's been great hearing you and talking to you. I need to leave now, as I have some things to do before going to our next appointment with some very good people, a young married couple who are excited to learn more about the gospel. We've sure had a wonderful conversation today."

Responding, Sarah says, "It surely has been wonderful. We've both enjoyed talking with you as well today. Keep up the great work, and we'll both be praying for you each day. Thanks so much for calling. Goodbye."

"Goodbye, Mom and Dad."

After the call, both Sarah and Wayne are looking at each other with much happiness showing on their faces. Sarah then asks, "Wow, Wayne, what do you think of our son now?"

"Sarah, he's such a spiritual person, just like you. I feel that he will be very successful in life. Now I can't wait to meet

Alexis. I'm so happy the Lord has brought us together."

"I am, too. Wayne, I'm feeling that Lexi may have some time to talk on the phone right now. I'll try calling her and see if she's available."

"That sounds good to me."

Sarah then calls Alexis and is excited when she answers. "Hello, is this Mom?"

"Hi, Lexi. I'm so glad you answered my call right now. Do you have some time to talk with me?"

"As a matter of fact, I do. I've been very busy with everything going on here, but you happened to call me at just the right time. Mom, I'm so excited! I've just been promoted to the position of head chef where I'm working. I'm receiving a huge raise as well. It'll easily pay off my student loan, as well as my car loan. Isn't that great?"

"It sure is, Lexi. I'm so proud of you! How are your studies going?"

"They're going super well. In fact, I'm actually ahead in two of my classes, and the administrators here have told me that they'll give me full credit for them, even though I'm finishing them right now. They're letting me add a couple more online classes in their place, and I can finish them as quickly as I want. I'll be getting my degree in no time. What do you think of that?"

"Lexi, that sounds so wonderful. You're pursuing what you really enjoy doing. I'm so happy for you. Lexi, I have some great news. I just finished talking with Ethan on the phone, and he's doing very well. He's a senior companion and is successfully teaching and helping many people there, including his new junior companion who has Asperger's Syndrome. How about that?"

"Wow, Mom, Ethan has certainly progressed well. Growing up together, I always felt he was and is a very special person. I felt such a strong need to help him and love him then, and the love he and you have shown me, along with Trish's, has also been a tremendous help to me. I'm so happy for him. I'm excited that he's finishing his mission well, and it'll be fun to see him when he comes home, as it will be for you."

"Yes, it will be exciting when he comes home, and you mentioned earlier that you will be able to come here briefly when he arrives, when I bring him home from the airport."

"That's right. I really want to see him when he first comes home. Keep me updated on the exact time, and I'll make time to drive down to the house and wait for you and Ethan to come."

"That will be great. Well, Lexi, I have some more news for you, which I believe you'll find very exciting."

"You do? What news is that, Mom?"

"Remember when I talked to you at times on the phone about this person I met at church a little over a year ago? Well, we've been getting to know each other better during this time, and something very special recently happened. Lexi, we both had a dinner here, and during our conversation the Lord's Spirit touched us very strongly, and both of us received the intense impression that we should be married in the temple. Lexi, Wayne Spencer and I are engaged to be married the third week after Ethan comes home."

"Oh, Mom, that's so wonderful to hear! I'm having a very good feeling about this. I know it is right for you and for us. Is he there with you right now?"

"Yes, Lexi. I have this on speaker. Here he is."

"Hi, Lexi. It's good to hear your voice, and it's great that you're doing so well. I'm very happy for you. It'll be fun to meet you when Ethan comes home. He knows about our wedding and is very happy for us. He also feels it's right."

"Ethan is such a great brother to me, and is a wonderful person. I just feel so strongly that we are meant to be a forever family together. It's so good to talk with you."

"It's great getting to know you, and I'm looking forward to seeing you in person. I can feel that you're a very spiritual member of the family, along with your mother and Ethan."

Sarah then comments, "Lexi, I know you also feel that Wayne is a very spiritual person. You see how the Lord's purposes work together for our good."

"Well, Mom, this has really made my day. I'd love to talk more, but I need to go now. You know how busy I am. I'm just so excited. Be sure to let me know when you'll be coming home with Ethan from the airport, and I'll be there. It's been fun talking to both of you. Goodbye, Mom and ... Dad."

After the call finishes, Wayne says with a bit of emotion, "Sarah, Lexi certainly is a very wonderful person, isn't she. I can really feel she will be successful in life."

"Thank you, Wayne. We'll be a great family together. Now, I can hardly wait for you to meet both of them in person. It will be a very happy day."

"It sure will. Thanks so much for letting me talk to both of them."

"You're very welcome, Wayne. You are such a wonderful person, and I'm so glad we were able to meet and get to know each other. We certainly have many blessings. Would you like to stay for dinner? We can talk more about our plans and about all the arrangements for our wedding."

"That will be so fun. Thank you, Sarah. I can help you with preparing dinner and give any other help you need."

"You're such a sweet person. I prayed many times that I would meet the right person for me, and here you are."

Wayne thanks Sarah and expresses his sincere appreciation for her. He embraces her and gives her a loving kiss. He helps her in the kitchen and they have a great dinner together. They spend a relaxing evening after their meal and after cleaning the kitchen. They watch a couple of very inspiring Church videos about Christ, which greatly invites the Lord's Spirit to be with them. He then thanks her and wishes her a wonderful evening before he leaves.

During the next few weeks, they are both busy preparing

for their wedding and the reception by making the necessary arrangements, scheduling the facilities, and making the temple appointment for their marriage there. He will also be receiving his own temple ordinances just before the marriage.

The time quickly arrives for Ethan to complete his mission. He calls and lets his mother know the time he will be arriving at the airport two days later. She then calls Alexis and lets her know the time that she and Ethan will be arriving at the house. Alexis is so excited and plans to be there an hour earlier. She is planning to come with a couple of her friends and set up some decorations to welcome him home.

In two days, Sarah and Wayne are eagerly waiting at the airport, watching for when his flight comes. It does, and they both are watching the passengers as they come around the corner, some of them to greet some of the others also waiting there. Then it happens. Ethan comes in view, all smiles, and quickly goes up to Sarah and embraces her. They are both so happy to see and hold each other after being apart for two years.

He exclaims, "Mom, I'm so happy to see you! I've had such a wonderful time, but it feels good to come home again." He notices Wayne standing there and asks, "Dad, is that you? I'm so happy to meet you."

Wayne joyfully responds, "I'm very happy to meet you, too. Ethan, I can feel such a great spirit about you, and I'm excited to get to know you better. It was so fun talking on the phone with you a while back, and it's great to see you now. You look so good."

"Well, I don't know if I look my best right now, after this long trip home, but you look great! It's so fun to see you, and I really feel something special about you. We have so much to talk about, and I'm looking forward to talking and knowing you better."

"Yes, it will also be fun to get to know more about you."

Sarah then says, "It's great that you enjoy each other so

much. There'll be plenty of time to talk. We need to go pick up your luggage now."

While walking to the baggage claim area, Sarah tells Ethan, "By the way, Lexi told me she'll be waiting for us at the house. She's so excited to see you."

"Oh, I'm so excited to see her again. She's such a good sister to me. I assume she is still doing well in school."

"Yes, she's doing very well. In fact, she's ahead in some of her classes, so it looks like she'll graduate sooner than we all first thought."

"That's great! She's always been very smart, and she loves cooking so much. She'll do wonderful, and I feel she'll be very successful. Well, it looks like this is my luggage right here. Dad, can you help me with this?"

"Certainly, Ethan. We'll get this all loaded up in the car, and we'll be on our way."

"Thanks, Dad."

With everything in the car, all three make the nearly two-hour drive to the house. When they arrive, they're all surprised to see the front of the house completely decorated with welcoming signs and banners, many balloons, and crepe paper hanging everywhere. They get out of the car, and before Sarah can say anything, Alexis comes running out of the house, goes right up to Ethan, puts both her arms around him, and exclaims, "Welcome home, Ethan! It's so fun to see you again after all this time! I just knew you could do this. I'm so very happy for you! Come inside. I have something very special for you."

Everyone goes into the house, only to encounter even more balloons and numerous other decorations. Alexis leads Ethan to the large kitchen counter, where he is very surprised to see a full sheet cake there, intricately and beautifully decorated with much artwork, and big, fancy lettering which says, "Welcome Home, Ethan – You're Fantastic!"

Ethan is so shocked that he stands there for a moment,

staring at it, unable to say anything. He then smiles at her and joyfully says, "Lexi, you're so sweet. Thank you very much! You're so good to me. Did you make all this yourself?"

"Most of it. My friends here helped with some of the artwork."

"Oh, I didn't notice both of you. Excuse me for walking right past you, but I was so taken in by what I saw here."

"Ethan, these are my two good friends from school, Hayley and Amber. They also helped me with the decorations."

"Good to meet you. Thanks for coming and helping Lexi with all this. I'm certainly very surprised. You are all so wonderful."

Alexis then suggests, "Everyone come in here and have a seat, and we'll serve all of you a piece of Ethan's 'Welcome Home' cake."

When they do, Alexis sees Wayne next to her mother and asks, "Dad, is that you?"

"Yes, I'm Wayne. I'm so happy to see you in person. I was so impressed when I talked with you on the phone. I can see you're a very special person, and I know you'll have a great future."

"Dad, that means so much to me. Thank you very much." She then hugs him, then hugs her mother and joyfully says, "Mom, it's fun to see you, too. This is really a great reunion we're having. This is a special day I'll always remember."

"It certainly is," responds Sarah. "I really enjoy seeing everyone together again."

The following Sunday, Ethan is scheduled to give his homecoming talk at church. Alexis is also able to be there. He gives a very spiritual message, along with impressive experiences he had while teaching the people in Argentina. He relates one in particular, where a family had an emotional experience after he and his companion gave their testimonies concerning the truthfulness of what they were teaching them. The entire family felt for certain that this information contains the truth which they were trying to find for a long time.

They all shed some tears of joy and expressed great smiles. After Ethan relates this story in its entirety, many of the people there listening to him are feeling very touched and rather emotional themselves. He finishes his talk on a very positive, spiritual note, and the Lord's Spirit is felt in an overwhelming manner by many.

When the meeting ends, he receives a great number of congratulations and acknowledgments of appreciation for his wonderful message. Sarah and Alexis are extremely happy for him as well, along with Wayne, and Sarah is nearly overcome with emotion when she expresses her gratitude for the great progression she has seen in him.

Three weeks later, the day arrives for Sarah and Wayne to be married. Sarah is using her vacation leave from her work during this time, so she has plenty of time to help with the preparation for this special day. Ethan has been helping both of them as well with their wedding preparations. He now has his driver's license, and has run a few errands for them, using a borrowed car. He is very excited for this special occasion, as well as being happy for both of them, and also knowing that his mother will now have more happiness in her life. As Alexis has a short break from school during this time, she is also able to assist in preparing everything for the reception, along with her two friends. She has prepared all the refreshments for the guests. Much of the setup is rented, and is being delivered to their reception venue, which is in a peaceful outdoor setting in the foothills, close to a river and surrounded by many trees. The reception will be held in the evening, and even though the date is a little past midsummer, it will be pleasantly comfortable there, a perfect evening.

That morning, Wayne and Sarah arrive at the temple for their wedding. As Ethan has already received his ordinances there, he will be Wayne's escort for when he receives his own. Ethan is very happy to do this, and is excited for him. After this occurs, it's time for their marriage. Some guests who know

Sarah from church have been invited, along with Ruth and Alice. They are all very happy to be there, and a few are inside the room to see Sarah become happily married. Sarah's friends are also excited for her. It is a very touching ceremony, where Sarah and Wayne become quite emotional as they strongly feel the Spirit there. Many show their appreciation for them in the foyer when it concludes. Many others are waiting outside to congratulate them when they come out, including Alexis and her friends. Several pictures are taken as well. David, Sarah's father, isn't able to be there, as his health is not quite what it used to be. However, Sarah calls him and tells him all about it afterward.

The wedding company and a few guests then go and have a great luncheon, which is enjoyed by everyone there. Wayne and Sarah go to their house afterward to relax and get ready for the reception. Wayne has a handsome tuxedo and Sarah has a very beautiful, exquisite wedding dress to wear at the reception. They're both so very excited and grateful for this special day.

Sarah joyfully tells him, "Wayne, we're now actually married. Isn't it wonderful?"

"It certainly is. I never dreamed I could ever be so happy as I am now. Sarah, honey, you're the jewel of my life."

"Thank you, honey. You're the righteous fortress in mine. Wasn't it so wonderful to feel the Spirit so strongly when we were being married?"

"It certainly was, and I still feel it intensely when I look into your eyes. I love you beyond what words can say."

"That is a beautiful compliment, and I feel it very strongly with you, too."

"Thank you. If you like, I'll help you try on your dress now and make sure everything is okay with it. How does that sound?"

"That sounds wonderful. I'd like to see you in your tux as well. It's going to be a great reception tonight. I'm really looking forward to it."

A couple of hours later, they are both dressed and ready to go to their reception. Ethan is nicely dressed as well, and will be Wayne's best man. Alexis is already there at the venue, putting the finishing touches on everything. Both Ethan and Alexis are so excited for their mom, and want to make sure that all goes perfectly for their special evening.

They arrive and are warmly welcomed by those already there. Alexis sees her mom in her beautiful wedding gown and can't believe her eyes. She exclaims, "Mom, you look just like a princess out of a fairy tale. You look marvelous!"

"Thanks, Lexi. I can see you're so happy for me. This is certainly going to be a great evening. You look very excited."

"I sure am. Did Ethan come with you?"

"Yes. He's over there, talking with your new dad."

"It'll sure be fun having a new dad. By the way, I guess your last name is now Spencer. And then when I'm married, my last name will change as well. I've been dating a little. There are a couple of great guys I'm slowly getting to know, and there's one in particular I like better. But I don't know just yet. I guess I'll feel it for certain when the time is right."

"You certainly will, Lexi. As you continue praying and staying close to the Lord, His Spirit will confirm to you what is right."

"Mom, you always seem to know just the right thing to say to me that makes me feel even better. You've helped me so much during my life. I just don't know how I can ever repay you." Her face shows a bit of emotion. "Thank you so much!"

"Don't worry about it, Lexi. Just know that I'll always love you." She gives Alexis a hug. "Oh, look, I think we're getting close to starting the reception. The music's already beginning as well. It sounds so beautiful; it makes me feel happy all over."

They go to their places, and the reception begins. Both Ruth and Alice are there, who talk with Sarah a little; they then talk some more later. They are both very excited to see

Ethan there, and they talk with him for quite a while, especially Alice. She is so thrilled, seeing how he has grown up like he has, and is now able to do so much more, including going on a mission. Alice tells him that she always felt that he would be able to do well in his life, for which he thanks her. Ruth also enjoys seeing him again, and is very happy to see how he has progressed so well. They both enjoy visiting with Alexis also, and are happy with her accomplishments. They spend some time talking with Wayne, getting to know him a little more, and are thankful that such a spiritual person is now in Sarah's life.

The reception is a beautiful experience, and is enjoyed by everyone there. Wayne and Sarah are especially happy, along with being very grateful for all the events transpiring that day. They're so excited for this opportunity to begin a new life together. After talking with many people there, the time comes for them to leave and begin their honeymoon. Everyone wishes them well and they all say goodbye as they leave.

They've made arrangements to go to a resort area not very far away, to spend a few relaxing days. During this time, Ethan and Alexis take care of the return and clean-up details, along with any other items needing attention. As this is occurring during the weekend, Alexis stays and spends some quality time with Ethan, each of them sharing precious stories and information involving their lives during the last two years. Alexis shares how the Lord has helped her in her studies and how thankful she is to Him for His assistance in helping her complete her classes rapidly. She shares how much she enjoys her work. Ethan expresses great appreciation to his sister for her accomplishments. He then shares with her some more touching stories and experiences he had during his mission, and how he felt the Lord's Spirit with him many times as he was teaching the people. After relating a very touching, spiritual experience he had, Alexis strongly feels the Spirit and becomes quite emotional. They hug each other and feel a special spiritual closeness. They continue conversing with each other as they share their Christlike love together.

The next day they both go to church and are very uplifted from the talks and teachings given there about the purpose of families. They come home feeling refreshed and are so grateful that they now have a loving father who will be with them forever. Thinking of this, and after mentioning it to each other, they feel very joyful and hug each other again.

They then realize that they're standing close to Trisha's photo, painting, and plaque. Alexis emotionally says, "Ethan, I feel that Trish is right here with us now, and that she's hugging us too. She's very happy about our new father and how we are becoming a forever family. I know she's also excited about what we've both accomplished."

"Lexi, I strongly feel this, also. Looking at the photo of her beautiful face reminds me again of her intense Christlike love she has for everyone. We're so blessed to have her as a member of our wonderful family. It will be a beautiful experience when we can see her again." Ethan's face is showing a sentimental look.

Alexis puts her arm around him and tearfully says, "It certainly will be. It's so great we're having this experience. Ethan, I love you so much!"

"You're such a great sister. I love you and really appreciate you. Thank you for all you do. I surely enjoy your cooking. I'm looking forward to a wonderful lunch and dinner."

"Well, I guess it's now lunchtime. Would you like to help me?"

"I sure would! It's so fun sharing this time together with you."

After enjoying this Sabbath day together, Alexis says goodnight to Ethan and leaves to go back to her own place, as she needs to return to work the next day at the restaurant where she is employed. Ethan is very thankful for having this special time to share with his sister.

The week passes and it's around the time when Wayne and Sarah are ready to return home from their honeymoon getaway. Ethan has been in contact with several of the Church ward members there and has been of service in any way he could during that week. He has kept all the wedding gifts there at the house for his parents, for them to open when they return. They do return Saturday afternoon, all excited and happy from having such a good time. They greet Ethan and decide to open their gifts right then. They're very excited again when they see some of the gifts which were given to them. A couple of them have a higher value, and a few are handmade, especially for the two of them. They're very grateful for the thoughtfulness of their friends.

The next day, they attend church with Ethan. Many of the ward members there congratulate Sarah and Wayne on their marriage, and sincerely wish them all the best in their new life together. Sarah thanks those members who know her very well, who gave some of the gifts to them. She tells them she's really appreciative of their thoughtfulness, and for their loving friendship they have for both of them. They respond to her and to Wayne in a positive manner, showing their excitement in this special occasion, knowing that Sarah deserves a good husband in her life.

Chapter Three
THE GREAT PATRIARCH

T HE next Monday, Sarah returns to her work as executive manager at the telephone consulting company. Wayne has a part-time job as a librarian in their city. He hasn't been very successful in finding a solid career in his life, but is happy doing his work where he is now. Sarah is very content continuing with her employment and doesn't mind the fact that her husband works only part-time. During that week, Ethan helps Wayne move all his belongings from his apartment to their house. Ethan is getting to know his new father even better now; they are very compatible together, which makes Ethan very happy.

A week later, Sarah comes home from her work very excited and asks Ethan to come hear what she has to say. He goes into their living room, wondering why she's so excited.

He curiously asks, "Mom, what's all your excitement about? Why are you so happy?"

"Ethan, I have good news for you. Remember when you asked me if I knew or heard of a good job opening for you? Well, I found out today at work that one of my workers is leaving. This creates an opening which needs to be filled right away. I thought of you first, as I feel you'll be perfect for it. How about it?"

"Mom, you're so wonderful!" Ethan exclaims. "I feel this will be just right for me. When do I begin?"

"You can come tomorrow morning for your orientation. Your group leader is a very nice person, and he will help you understand everything you need to know. You enjoy working with computers, so I feel you'll pick that up very quickly. This will be a full-time job, so you'll be able to save good money for your future."

"This is exciting. I know I'll do great work there. Thank you so much!"

The next morning, Sarah and Ethan go to their place of work, and Sarah introduces him to everyone. They're pleased that he will be a good worker, and he's excited to get to know some of the other workers, along with learning his new responsibilities. He doesn't mind making the forty-minute trip with his mother to work there each day.

It turns out that Ethan is a very good fit for this position. He is learning his job description extremely well, and is very proficient and works in a good, expedient manner. Along with his group leader, Sarah is also pleased with his performance, and tells him that he has a good future there.

After a month, some tremendously exciting news comes from the company headquarters. One member of the board of directors calls and makes an appointment to come and meet with Sarah at her place of work. On the day of the appointment, two members of the board come and meet with her in a meeting room.

After kindly greeting her, one of them says, "Sarah, we have seen your excellent performance as executive manager here at this center. My colleague here is retiring in three weeks, and we feel that you are the best candidate to fill his position. So, we are offering you the opportunity to become a member of the board of directors for our corporation. What are your thoughts about it?"

Looking a little stunned, she responds, "I ... I don't know what to say. You really feel I'm the best qualified person to fill the position?"

"Yes, we do. You will be able to remain here and continue your excellent work as executive manager in this building, but you will have some additional responsibilities as a director, and there will be a few meetings to attend at corporate head-quarters. You'll also receive an increase in your pay. Do you have an answer now, or would you like to take a day to think about it?"

"I would like to do it, but can I let you know tomorrow morning?"

"That will be fine. Here's my contact information. For your information, this position will begin three weeks from tomorrow. If you decline, we have another person in mind, but he's not nearly as good as you are. People like you are hard to find. You'll be doing us a great favor if you accept. You're a tremendous asset to our corporation."

"Thank you very much for your compliment. I believe I will accept the position, but I will tell you for certain tomor-row morning, if that's alright."

"Great! I'm looking forward to your call. It's been a plea-sure meeting with you."

They both shake hands with her as they all stand. They wish her a great day as they leave the room. She goes to her own office and begins her work, feeling very good about what just occurred.

After finishing work for the day, as they are traveling home, Sarah tells Ethan about the offer from company head-quarters. He's very excited for her and tells her that she should take it. She agrees with him, now feeling even better about it. Suddenly, they hear an extremely loud thump which great-ly startles them, immediately followed by a very loud, rapid thumping under the car. Sarah stops the car off the side of the road. They get out and find a rear tire has blown. Ethan helps his mother change it; they then go to a good tire center to buy a replacement, which is installed. This particular time, they have no means of informing Wayne about what has occurred.

The delay in arriving home is causing Wayne to wonder what has happened to them, but he is relieved after finding out that all is now fine. He's very excited when Sarah tells him about the offer at work. He tells her it's okay with him to go ahead and accept the offer, which she now definitely feels comfortable doing.

The next morning, she calls and lets them know that she is accepting the offer of her new position. The other directors are very pleased with her decision and inform her of her first meeting with them before she assumes her position on the board of directors.

A month later, Sarah is very pleased fulfilling the responsibilities in her new position, along with her current responsibilities as supervisor/executive manager where she presently works. All is going well, until she receives a phone call from her uncle, Richard, out of state. Her father, David, is living with him, and he is now calling her to inform her that David's health is declining. He informs her that he is becoming David's caregiver, and has needed to take him to the medical center once to receive new prescription medications and further assistance. He tells her that it would be a good idea to come and visit him, as he feels that David's health will continue to decline rather quickly.

Sarah is distraught about this. She thanks him for calling and letting her know, and says that she will go see him. She lets Alexis know about this, who is also saddened on hearing this news. She isn't able to take a break from her classes right now, but she asks her mom to keep her updated on the latest happenings. She tells her mom that she will be praying for him as well, for which Sarah thanks her.

Sarah arranges to take a week off from work, along with Ethan, so that they will have time to travel and see David. Due to this urgent need, one of the directors comes and fills in for her. When Sarah and Ethan arrive, after traveling for an entire day, they are saddened to know that David is even more bedridden now, as he has become worse these last two days.

After greeting her uncle, they go into David's room, and see him lying in his bed. Sarah gently asks, "Dad, how are you feeling? You look like you're uncomfortable."

He replies, "Oh, Sarah, I'm so glad you came to see me. You, too, Ethan. Quite a bit has happened since I last saw you. I'm having my difficulties, but I'm okay." He grimaces as he tries to adjust himself in the bed. He shows an emotional expression on his face and says, "Sarah, I'm dying. The doctor tells me I have a rare condition which is causing my body to slowly stop functioning. It's worse now."

Ethan gives his grandfather a hug. He tearfully says, "Grandfather, I don't want you to go yet. You mean so much to me. You've been there with us many times in our lives." He pauses and intensely looks at his grandfather's face for a moment as Sarah is watching them. He continues. "You helped me in such a special way at Trish's funeral. I couldn't have been able to get through that time without you. You told me some comforting things then, which all came true. You dedicated her grave, saying some very promising words about her, including some great blessings which I know will happen." He sheds a couple more tears, thinking about this. "Grandfather, you ordained me an Elder in the Church, giving me very promising blessings, some of which are mentioned in my patriarchal blessing, which you didn't know were there beforehand. You told me how you think I'm a special person, when you looked at me when I was young, that I have a special mission to fulfill. You've been, and are such a great patriarch in our family, and I can feel the Spirit of the Lord very strongly with you. Grandfather, I ... want you to stay with us as long as you can. Please ... you mean so much to me." Ethan is now very tearful.

David looks emotionally at Ethan. He tells him, "Ethan, you mean very much to me, too. I sincerely appreciate all you said to me. Ethan, remember, our Savior has His specific plan for each one of us. I am now fulfilling His plan for me. I have felt my wife's presence with me more, along with Trisha's. Remember, we are all an eternal family, where we are able to all live lovingly together forever. You know how being separated from a loved one when that person passes to the other side causes much sadness and grieving, and that's normal, because that's showing your sincere expression of tremendous love for that person. Remember what I told you at Trisha's passing, that our Savior will help you, and you can feel His presence with you all the time. You still have a tremendous mission to fulfill in this life, as well as after this life, and I still know that you will be receiving great blessings, beyond your comprehension. You have already seen this to a small degree during your mission for the Church. I know through the Spirit that what I've said is completely true."

Both Ethan and Sarah show more tender feelings, after hearing David's sweet words to Ethan. Sarah takes her father's hand in hers and tenderly says, "Dad, remember at Mom's passing, when you told me you felt that it was the Lord's time for her?" He looks at her and smiles. "I also felt it, and I'm now feeling more about the Lord's will for you, even though it's difficult. Yes, you are a great patriarch in our family, and you will continue to be. You've been a true father to me all my life, and you are a very positive example to everyone. We will miss you, but like you've always taught us, we will all be a forever family. I've been married in the temple to a wonderful, new husband, who is very faithful, and we have been sealed together. It was such a great experience, and it's a wonderful feeling knowing this, that the Lord's promises are true as we continue to follow Him. Dad, I love you so very, very much."

Suddenly, David's body begins to quiver, which gradually increases. Sarah quickly calls out to her uncle to call 9-1-1, which he does. David's convulsions are increasing more when the ambulance arrives a minute later. The paramedics immediately take him and put him into the ambulance, and they treat him as they quickly go to the hospital. The other three go in Sarah's car, and arrive there some minutes later. They are asked to stay in a waiting area, to be notified when they are allowed to enter.

Half an hour passes and they are very concerned. Sarah says a prayer in her heart that all will go okay, and that the Lord will comfort them. Ethan is holding his mom's hand. A few minutes later, the ER doctor comes out and tells them that David just passed away, that they did all they could to keep him alive. Ethan cries out a bit, and Sarah is weeping many tears. They both hug each other tightly for a few minutes, while her uncle has his arm around them.

Sarah quietly says, between sobs, "Yes, I know our Savior knows what He's doing."

Her uncle, Richard, then tearfully says, "He's been such a tremendous older brother to me. He's been such a great help and a good example. I'll greatly miss him."

Sarah then goes and asks one of the medical staff when they can see him. The staff member leads them into the room, where Sarah sees a peaceful expression on her father's face. She looks at him for a moment, then suddenly experiences a very special feeling about her.

She tenderly says, "I feel my Dad's arms around me right now, and I feel he's telling me that things are fine, that he's in a very happy, beautiful place, and that he's feeling great joy. I also feel he's rejoicing to be with my mother again, who is right here, and that he's with a very, very loving spirit person, who I know for certain is Trish. I feel he's telling me that everything will be okay and to keep having faith. Now, I feel he's gone to meet some other people. Ethan, Uncle Richard, I know more definitely that we are becoming a forever family, that we will see them again and be together with them."

Ethan emotionally responds, "Mom, it's so wonderful you just had that experience. It confirms to me even more the reality of the Spirit World, and that everything Christ has taught us is definitely true, and we are on the road to receiving blessings beyond our comprehension."

Richard then responds while showing some emotion. "I understand more about what you two are saying. It's now making more sense to me."

Sarah then says, "This is all true. Well, I need to call the mortuary back home to make the arrangements. Don't worry, Uncle Richard, I can now take care of the funeral expenses, and we can bring you with us and I'll pay for your trip back home. It will be fine."

All arrangements are made, and David's body is transferred to the mortuary in Sarah's first city, where David and his wife, Carol, originally lived. The three travel there, and plan to notify Alexis and Ruth about the recent events. The next day, they all go to visit with Alexis personally at the university, to share with her the news of David's passing. She feels very heartbroken, but then feels much better after Sarah and Ethan share all what was said, including the wonderful experiences they had there. She is excited as she meets her great uncle. They then proceed to plan the funeral together. Alexis plans to take leave from her classes and studies during the time of the funeral. The three then travel back to go visit Ruth.

Upon arriving, Ruth answers the door and is very pleasantly surprised to see Sarah and Ethan there, along with Richard. She gasps, and excitedly says, "Come in, come in, Sarah and Ethan. What a pleasant surprise! It's great to see you again after your wedding. Come, sit down. Who is this you brought with you?"

"Ruth, this is my uncle, Richard." They both shake hands. "He's here because ... well, I have some sad news. My father just passed on, and we are in the process of planning his funeral."

"Oh, Sarah, I'm so sorry to hear that. I know he's a very spiritual person. I knew that when I first met him at Trisha's funeral. It must be very hard on you."

"Well, yes, but the Lord has greatly helped me through this. I feel such a wonderful peacefulness. Our Savior's plans for us are simply marvelous."

"I agree. Sarah, you do look very content. Ethan, it's good to see you again. How are you making it through all this?"

"Actually, I'm doing okay. My grandfather gave me a very precious message just before his passing, which I will always treasure. I definitely know that our families can go on forever. Ruth, I know it. I *will* see him again, and he will be in our family."

"Ethan, it's good to see you thinking so positively. I can surely see the change in you after fulfilling your Church mission." Ruth's face shows some sadness. She looks at them and continues, "I just don't know about my family. All I have is my sister, Esther. No children, no husband, and my parents are not members, and my father has already passed away. I don't see much hope for a forever family with me. Nothing has improved." Ruth lowers her head a little and sheds a couple of tears. "Sarah, is there any hope for me?"

"Ruth, there certainly is! Just keep praying and having faith, and the Lord's promises and blessings will be with you as much as anyone else who follows Him."

Ethan then interjects with, "Ruth, this is a great faith-building experience for you. Our Savior knows what He is doing. I know He has a great plan for you."

"Thank you, Ethan. You've certainly grown. I love the change I see in you, and I can feel the Spirit with you." Ruth shows a small smile and she continues. "The spiritual feeling I now have reminds me of the special experiences I had with Trisha, which are indelibly imprinted in my being. She taught me so much about Christ and who He really is, that I now feel that Christ does have a special plan for me. Thank you both for helping me feel better."

"You're very welcome," Sarah responds. "You're a very special person. Ruth, it's up to you, but would you feel like speaking at my father's funeral?"

"Knowing your father, and how special he is, I would love to speak at his funeral. I think that he would want me to, as well."

"Thank you, Ruth. I appreciate your willingness to do this. We need to go now. I'll let you know the exact day it will be held. The location is their former ward building. Here's the address to it. It's been fun talking with you."

"Yes, it's been fun. I'm glad you came. You all helped me feel better today. It's been good meeting you, Richard."

Sarah comments, "My uncle's not much of a talker, but he enjoys the company."

Richard then says, "It's been a pleasure getting to know you, Ruth."

They all shake hands and then leave Ruth's place. They travel home and inform Wayne that Richard will be staying with them until the funeral is completed. He understands and is happy to meet Richard and to know him better. Sarah has been keeping her husband informed of all the happenings, and he offers his condolences to her.

Sarah works out the details with the mortuary and plans the date for the funeral. She gives out the invitations to the many who knew him before he moved. Alexis will be one of the speakers, along with Ethan and Ruth. Wayne will read his life sketch. Richard agrees to give a short talk honoring his brother, along with offering the family prayer. Sarah has prepared a very spiritual talk to honor her father.

The day of the funeral comes, and everything goes very well. It turns out to be a rather spiritual service, where many people who knew him are very touched with what is said. Afterward, they go to the cemetery, where Ethan dedicates the grave. It is an emotional experience for him, knowing all that David had done for him throughout his life.

They come back and have a good luncheon; then Alexis returns to her place after saying goodbye to Ruth, who then says her goodbyes before going home. Richard is taken to the airport for his return trip home. Wayne, Sarah, and Ethan travel to their house, and are exhausted in more ways than one. The following Monday, Sarah and Ethan return to their work, and are able to resume their duties rather well; however, the loss of David in their lives is still quite fresh on their minds, and at times they both experience short bouts of grieving. They each say a quick, silent prayer when this happens, to help themselves through these times.

Chapter Four

THE CONTRIBUTION

A few months later, Sarah feels prompted to call Alice on her phone again. She wasn't available to come at the time of David's passing, and hasn't heard from her since that time.

Alice answers the call, and Sarah says, "Hello, Alice. I haven't talked with you for a while. Just wondering how you're doing?"

She responds, "Sarah, I'm doing okay, but I seem to be a bit slower now. I'm a little past retirement age, but I want to continue working. However, I've been having some difficulties remembering everything, and my doctor says I might have an issue with my brain. He's given me some supplements to help me with this, but he thinks I might have to retire from my occupation I love so much."

"Alice, I'm sorry to hear that things are not quite the same as they were, but we know things change when we age. It was a shock to me about my father's passing, but I know the Lord has His plan for each of us."

"Thanks for your thoughts, Sarah. How is Ethan doing now?"

"Oh, Alice, he's doing extremely well. His Church mission has really helped him. He's quite a spiritual person, and you wouldn't even know he has Asperger's. His autistic characteristics are mostly gone. Once in a while he needs a little explanation to understand certain social situations, but other than that, he's doing very well. Our Savior certainly has His plan for him."

"You say I wouldn't know he has Asperger's and he's doing very well? Sarah, you know he has Asperger's Syndrome. I'm not sure what you're telling me, or if I understand you."

"Alice, I think your doctor is correct. I can tell something is happening to your brain. I believe you do need to retire, and your doctor may need to help you some more."

"You really think so? Well, I'll see how it goes. I need to go now. Thanks for calling me. I'll talk with you later."

"Okay, Alice. Goodbye."

As Sarah is very concerned about Alice's responses, she obtains the information for Alice's local Church leaders, and speaks with a couple of them about her condition. She tells them that she's a close friend to Alice. They each say that they will check on her and let Sarah know what they find.

A few days later, one of them calls Sarah and tells her that Alice has another appointment scheduled with her doctor. He says there are a couple of members in her Church ward there who are assigned to check with her and make sure she is okay. Sarah asks him to keep her updated on this situation. He tells her that he will.

The ward member who was first assigned to check on Alice calls Sarah the following Monday. He sounds very concerned. He asks, "Sarah, how long have you known Alice?"

She replies, "Oh, it's been a very long time, over thirty years. She's been a close family friend all these years. Why?"

"Well, it looks like she needs some help. She's been to the doctor, who then had a hospital specialist do some testing on her brain. Sarah, it's been confirmed that Alice is in the early stages of dementia, and the indications are that it's progressing a bit faster than usual. Our ward leader here is working with the directors of her counseling group to put in her immediate retirement. She does have a brother who lives much farther away. Since you're the closest contact, you'll need to come and help with the paperwork, and to indicate that you are the responsible person. She will need to go to a care center, and she will need your input and assistance with this. I'm sorry to be the bearer of bad news, but this is requiring immediate attention."

"This is difficult to hear about her. She's been such a tremendous help to us, and especially for my son. It's sad to know this is happening to her. When should I come?"

"Come as soon as you can, tomorrow if you are able."

"I will put in leave from my work for a week, but that's all I'll be able to do right now, as I'm director/manager in my company, and I've recently had to take some leave already. I can come again on an additional weekend, if necessary."

"That sounds fine." He gives Sarah the address and the additional information she needs when she arrives.

Sarah tells Wayne and Ethan the news about Alice. Ethan is heartbroken when he hears that Alice has dementia. He tearfully responds, "Alice has been such a tremendous help for me in my life. It's hard to know that she has this affliction now. I wish the best for her, and I'll pray for her as well."

Sarah then explains, "I'll need to make that long trip there tomorrow, and assist with her retirement papers and in securing a care center for her. I will be gone for a week, so Ethan, I need you to cover some of my responsibilities at work. I've already shown you some of this, and you can call me on my phone if you need more assistance. I know you can do this. I'll keep you updated about Alice."

"Okay, Mom, I feel this will work. Thanks for having such faith in me. I wish you a safe trip, and I'll be praying for Alice and for you."

"Thank you very much, Ethan. I know I can depend on you. Thank you for being who you are."

Early the next morning, Sarah leaves to go see Alice and her ward leaders there. Wayne takes Ethan to work in his car, then runs some errands. As this is a longer commute, he does some shopping there just before getting Ethan to come home in the evening. Meanwhile, Sarah arrives past midmorning after traveling almost 300 miles, to meet Alice's Church ward leader in his home. He and his family are keeping Alice there, in their guest bedroom, as she is experiencing periods of incoherence. Sarah fills out her necessary information on the retirement paperwork he has there, then is directed to Alice's room.

Sarah goes in and greets her, while she is resting on her bed. She looks up and says, "Sarah, is that you?"

"Yes, it's me. Do you know what's been happening? Do you know that you need to retire from your work now?"

"I think so. At times I wake up, and I realize I'm somewhere else than where I thought I was. This is so strange."

"I know. Do you remember being told why this is happening to you?"

"I think so. Something to do with my brain. Oh, I remember now. I was talking to you on the phone at my work, and you said something is wrong with me, but I don't remember what. Then I remember a neighbor taking me to the doctor, and now I'm here in my other neighbor's house. I'm not sure why. Can you tell me?"

"Alice, your brain is starting to develop some problems, which are now causing you to not remember everything that's happening. That's why you need to retire. Do you remember my mother?"

"Oh, yes, Sarah. Your mother is Carol. We were very close, and we worked in family counseling. I remember now. Carol did much research about developmental brain disorders, and I learned a lot from her. Yes, you have a son named Ethan, and

I remember diagnosing him with Asperger's Syndrome. It's all coming back to me. Ten years later, all of you came here to my office to meet Robert. I could see he helped Ethan in a great way. But it's very foggy with what's happening now. I don't know what's going on."

"Alice, it's good your long-term memory is still here. To help you now, you will be moving into a place where some very kind people will be helping you with your needs. They will be giving you your meals, and they will help you feel as comfortable as they can. We want you to enjoy your life as much as possible. I will be helping you get settled. You've known me for many, many years, so you'll be able to remember me the best. Everything will be okay. You know our Savior is helping you, too. Remember to pray."

"Thank you, Sarah. I know that prayer is very important, and I will keep praying."

Sarah tells Alice that she will be back, and then goes to talk to the ward leader about the care centers in the area. She reviews the information he has obtained, and goes to check out the three best centers she has selected. After doing this, one impresses her much more than the others. She goes back and tells them that she has a friend with dementia, and is working on getting her retirement income finalized, to pay for her stay there. They tell Sarah that they'll be happy to care for her there, and that they have a nice room all ready.

She goes back to the leader's house, and informs him of the plan. She stays there in the city for the next few days to finalize Alice's retirement arrangement with the major counseling group where she has been working, and to set up the Social Security payments and healthcare insurance. This is quite an involved process, but Sarah doesn't mind doing all this work, as she knows Alice deserves it.

After the week has passed, everything is set up with the care center; and the ward leader, along with a few others, help to move Alice and her belongings to the center. Sarah stays with her the first day at the care center, to help her become adjusted there, and to introduce her to the friendly workers who will be helping her each day. Alice is grateful to Sarah for doing this, and says that she now feels more comfortable. Sarah tells Alice that she has to return home the next morning, and that everything will be okay. She also tells her that she will call her on the phone a few times each week, to keep a close connection with her, explaining that she is a person she knows very well. She says goodbye and wishes her well.

The next morning, Sarah makes the long trip back home, and arrives later in the afternoon. An hour later, Wayne and Ethan arrive, after the commute from Ethan's work. Ethan doesn't have his own vehicle yet, but is planning to have one soon, as he already has his own driver's license. Both are happy to see Sarah back home, and are glad that she has been safe. They had picked up some dinner on the way home, so all three enjoy their meal together. Sarah then relaxes in the living room and tells them more of what occurred, and how she felt the Lord's guidance in much of what she did, after offering many prayers. She tells them that Alice feels very comfortable in her care center.

Sarah then asks Ethan how his work went during the past week. He responds with, "Mom, it went very well. The computer programs you use are very easy to understand, and the directions and information you left for me are simple to use. Thanks for explaining some of it to me earlier. It makes good sense to me, and I can help you even more in the future. Everything went so smoothly, and I had simple answers when the workers had questions which came up. I really enjoy working there."

"That's wonderful, Ethan. I'm so happy you enjoy your work. I will highly recommend you for the managerial position when the time comes."

"Thanks, Mom. You're the best in the world, along with my new dad and Lexi."

Sarah then tells them about something very interesting she found, while they were moving some of Alice's belongings from her apartment to the care center. She found a box containing much of the work and studies her mother, Carol, had accomplished in those earlier years. It also contains a great amount of work and information which Alice had compiled, unknown to Sarah, continuing Carol's studies about various brain disorders.

Sarah isn't sure if the corresponding national organizations have this information, so she contacts them and discovers they are lacking the research information which Alice acquired. Sarah discovered that Alice also stored much of her work in electronic format, so she gives the new information to them, for which they are extremely grateful. Each of them tells Sarah that they are very happy for this great contribution, that it will greatly expedite the assistance they offer to those needing their help. Sarah is very glad that Alice was able to accomplish this work to help others, before the onset of her illness.

Sarah keeps up with making regular telephone contact with Alice, who really appreciates her doing this. Alice sees Sarah as a very special friend, as she was with Sarah's mother, Carol, for many years. A few months later, Sarah notices that Alice is becoming less coherent while conversing on the phone with her, so she feels that it's very important for everyone to go visit her, before her now diagnosed Alzheimer's worsens. She plans a time when she and Ethan can take some vacation leave, and when Alexis has a break from school. She also invites Ruth, who is very excited to join all of them. Ruth has been living alone and feeling a bit depressed; however, she has been going to church and has talked with her sister, Esther, as well as frequently visiting the Loveless family who moved into Sarah's former house. They have been longtime friends with Esther.

On this beautiful morning, Alexis travels down to join her

family. Wayne, Sarah, and the two children travel in her new SUV to get Ruth, who is very ready. She's extremely excited to join them. Sarah then announces that they are going to see Robert, who lives on their way during this long journey. She is planning to bring him along as well.

They leave on their journey. Having made previous arrangements with Robert, they all stop in at his house to visit for a short time before bringing him along. When he opens the door, Ethan immediately goes up to him and exclaims, "Robert!" and gives him a hug.

Robert invites everyone in and says, "Hello, everyone. It's so good to see all of you again." Noticing Sarah's arm around Wayne, he asks, "Sarah, is this your new husband?"

"Yes, he is. This is Wayne." Robert shakes hands with him. "And this is Ruth, a very good friend of ours." He then shakes her hand.

"Glad to meet each of you. Ethan and Alexis, it's so good to see you again. You're all grown up now and looking very happy. Ethan, it's great that you're doing so well. I'm so happy to have been able to help you."

Ethan shows a bit of emotion on his face, and responds, "I'll always remember the wonderful time I had when we met with you, and you gave us such an inspiring presentation. You truly helped me change my life." He gives him another hug.

"Thank you very much, Ethan. It was such a pleasure helping you. I understand we're all going to see Alice. Sarah, you told me she isn't doing well. How is she now?"

Sarah sadly responds, "Oh, Robert, she isn't well at all. She has increasing Alzheimer's, and she may not remember you. She still knows me because I've been talking on the phone with her, and she's seen me recently. We're all going to visit her at the care center."

"I'm sorry to hear that. She was such a wonderful person when I came to know her at church. She especially enjoyed my presentation I gave the three of you. But, we know that people have to experience what the Lord has planned for them. I'll be praying for her."

Alexis then comments, "It'll be hard to see her like this now. I remember how excellent she was when you, Robert, gave us that wonderful presentation. You and Alice sure helped us more than anything else. It really changed Ethan's life. I'm so grateful for what you did." She sheds a couple of tears while looking at Robert.

"Thank you so much, Alexis. I'm excited that you're all happy with my efforts to help the three of you." Robert smiles while saying this.

Ruth and especially Wayne are a bit confused of what Robert actually did to help Ethan. Sarah explains to them, "You both know that Ethan has Asperger's Syndrome, and had a difficult time when he was growing up. Well, Robert also has Asperger's, and has learned how to practically overcome all aspects of it, and he shared his exciting and inspirational information with us after Alice informed us about him and planned a meeting with him. This effected a major change in Ethan, and you see he now functions much like Robert does. Wayne, honey, Alice originally diagnosed Ethan's Asperger's Syndrome while she was a certified therapist, and she's been a great help to us."

"So Robert is autistic as well?" Wayne asks. "It's very interesting to see how well Robert and Ethan have overcome the characteristics of their disorders and function so well."

"Yes, and Alice was very impressed with how both of them are now able to function in life. This is part of the information she preserved."

Everyone stays and talks for a few more minutes, then Sarah tells them that they need to continue on their journey. They go and enjoy lunch at a nice restaurant, then continue traveling to the care center. They arrive and are warmly greeted, then are led to Alice's room. They go in and Alice is lying on her bed, surprised at the large group of people coming to see her.

She recognizes Sarah and asks, "Sarah, is that you? Who are all these people?"

"Yes, Alice, it's me, Sarah. This is my family, and a couple of friends. We're here to visit with you for a little while, if that's okay."

"They can visit me, but I'd like to know who these people are." Alice is looking at them with a very confused look. Ethan and Alexis show some shock on their faces, seeing that Alice doesn't recognize them. They feel a bit sad about her present condition.

Sarah responds, "Alice, this is Ethan, and this is Alexis. This person over here is Robert. We were all together that Christmas season when Robert gave us that beautiful presentation to help Ethan overcome his Asperger's Syndrome. Do you remember how you showed us those great videos during our meeting then?"

"Yes, I think I remember that meeting we had, and showing the videos, but I don't recognize all of you. So this is Ethan, Alexis, and Robert. It's good to see you."

"Alice, this is Wayne, my new husband. He's a wonderful person, and a great member of our forever family. Over here is Ruth, my special friend who has helped me over the years. We all want to visit with you and help you feel happy. You have many friends."

"Okay, it will be fun to talk."

They visit Alice for a little while, then Sarah notices that she's becoming very tired, and suggests that they end the visit and leave. They all get up, say goodbye to Alice, then go outside. Ethan and Alexis note how they are very sad to see Alice in her present condition. Alexis sadly says, "I wish Alice could feel better. It's hard to see her like this."

Robert responds, "I understand. We know that people have to experience various types of trials in their lives. However, as a matter of fact, these trials are for their good. Alice will be a wonderful person in her life after this life; she will be very happy, and she will be helping many people."

Ethan and Alexis feel more comforted, hearing what Robert just told them. Ruth also feels that special comfort, and wants to visit with him more often. Wayne has especially enjoyed all the conversation, and wants to spend more time all together.

Sarah suggests that they all go to the same elite, high-end restaurant where she and her two children went to have dinner after Robert's presentation to them during that particular Christmas season. They go, and Alexis is excited to see that they've added some new gourmet dishes to their menu, and she takes notes. Everyone is very pleased with the food there that evening, and they have great conversations in a relaxed atmosphere, while Wayne and Ruth are becoming closer friends with Robert. He shares more inspirational information with all of them, which helps them feel very good about each of their lives.

Afterward, they start traveling back. They leave Robert at his home, who sincerely thanks them for their company and for the delicious meals. He shows his gratitude to each of them for being who they are. They all say goodbye and leave. Sarah is driving, and the others are conversing more about what has been said and what has taken place. They talk about the life Alice has now, and how difficult it must be for her. Sarah tells them that they should all pray for her, that she'll be comfortable. They all agree.

Alexis then changes the subject, and says that she felt something when they were having dinner at the fancy restaurant. She says, "I've been making similar dishes as head chef at the restaurant where I'm working. I feel that I can make these on my own, maybe some even better ones. When I graduate, I think I can save enough money to open my own place that people will love. I'll call it, 'Lexi's Gourmet Kitchen.' What do you all think?"

"Lexi, that'll be wonderful," responds Sarah. "Working in

something you enjoy is the best way to live your life, along with the Lord's help."

Ethan happily says, "I know you can do it, Lexi. You're very good at what you do, and I just can't wait for you to have your own business. It'll be so good there."

Ruth then comments, "I'd love to eat there, too. You made such great meals when you were still living at home, and I was there visiting. I wish I could eat your food all the time. It's so good."

"Thanks for your compliments. I feel more encouraged now. Oh, by the way, I have something else to tell you. Mom, you know I've been dating while I've been at school. Well, I've met this cutest boy there, whom I've been dating more. He's very strong in the Church, and I feel he may be getting ready to propose to me soon. What do you think?"

"Oh, Lexi, that's so wonderful!" exclaims Sarah. "Things are going very well for you. Be sure to keep us updated."

"I sure will, Mom. Actually, I'll be graduating in a few months, and I think I will start doing some graduate work in my culinary field. I'm paid very well where I work, and I don't have any debts at all. I'll have enough saved to pay for my studies, plus to put a good down payment on a place for my restaurant. I owe it all to our Savior. I know as I stay close to Him as you have taught me, He will bless me in my good endeavors."

Sarah is showing a bit of emotion, hearing her daughter's words. She feels very comforted, knowing the successful lives her two children are having. Wayne also feels very happy for them, and blessed to have them in the family.

Ruth then comments, "Sarah, I can surely feel the Spirit in your family. I have enjoyed being your friend all these years, but I still wish I could have the blessing of having a great family like you do." A few tears form in Ruth's eyes.

Sarah then feels prompted to say, "Ruth, it will be rather late when we arrive home. Would you like to stay in our guest room for a few days? I feel you need to talk some more."

Responding, she says, "Sarah, that's just what I need. How did you know?"

"The Spirit of the Lord guides us in many ways. Our Savior will also guide you. We can talk more about it later."

Alexis then says, "We can all talk together, if you want. I'll be staying at the house as well, because I'm on my break from school, and I'm taking some vacation leave from my work. I'll make you some of my extra delicious, fancy meals. I know you'll enjoy that."

Ruth excitedly responds, "I surely will. Thanks for everything you all do for me. I really feel all your love."

Chapter Five
RUTH'S SPECIAL JOURNEY

EVERYONE arrives late at Wayne and Sarah's house. Sarah prepares the guest room, and they all get ready to retire for the night. Sarah has what Ruth needs to sleep there, as well. Everyone sleeps very well that night, and they feel rejuvenated in the morning.

They wake up to a delightful aroma coming from the kitchen, including the distinct sweet aroma of bacon. Alexis has awakened early, wanting to surprise everyone with a gourmet breakfast. They are all surprised. They get themselves dressed and ready, and go into the dining room, where Alexis has the table beautifully set. She brings in each of their meals, and Wayne says a prayer of grace and blessing on their food, thanking Alexis for all her work and thoughtfulness.

They begin eating, and Ruth immediately starts beaming. She excitedly says, "Lexi, this is so tasty. It's simply wonderful. What a great gift you have. It's so fun to be able to have your food to eat. You prepare it so well!"

"Thank you, Ruth. That means a lot to me. I really enjoy helping people feel happy by doing what I enjoy doing. Mom, if it's okay with you, I'd like to make all our meals while I'm here. What do you think?"

"Lexi, you're the best in the world," responds Sarah. "I'm very much in agreement with it, and I'm sure everyone else is as well." The other three nod their approval. "Just let me know what you need at the store, and I can help you with it."

"Thanks, Mom, you can help at times if you like, but I can get much of it myself. I really enjoy doing it. This is my gift to all of you." Alexis is showing a great smile.

Sarah looks very happy. "Thank you very much, Lexi. You're such a sweet person. You'll do very well in your life. I just know it."

Wayne and Ethan are also very happy with Alexis and the great breakfast she prepared. They thank her afterward. Ruth gives her a very sincere, heartfelt compliment, including how happy she is to have her as a friend. Ruth remembers the excellent food she prepared some years ago, and is excited to have more of her delicious meals for the next few days.

After finishing and cleaning up, they all have a family prayer and do some scripture study together. Wayne and Ethan then go and work on a wood project and he shows Ethan about it, as Wayne loves woodworking. Alexis goes to a couple of food stores to get some less common ingredients she needs for the meals she is planning, along with other food items. Ruth feels this will be a good time to talk to Sarah about some important items in her life.

She asks, "Sarah, could we go somewhere alone, so we can talk for a while?"

Seeing the concern on Ruth's face, she responds, "Sure we can. Let's go to my office room."

They go in and Sarah closes the door. They sit down in some comfortable chairs. Ruth begins with, "Sarah, it's been good getting to know the Loveless family, who moved into your former house. They're good people, and I sit with them at church each Sunday. They've become good friends with me, and we visit when we can. I've been able to help them at times, but they're very busy, and there are not many others who want to take time to talk with me. I feel this is partly due to the fact that I'm African-American, and some people seem to be uncomfortable around me. Sarah, what do you think about that?"

"Sad to say, I know that some people are uncomfortable with certain races, but you know that I'm friendly with any-one, and I want to help everyone feel happy. There's a Japanese family in my ward who've told me they feel a bit out of place at times. They're very good people and I've welcomed them, and they feel I'm one of their best friends. Ruth, you are my very special friend, and you've helped me more than you realize. It doesn't matter to me where you come from; it matters who you really are, and I see that you're a very kind-hearted person who loves to help others. I'm so glad that you're one of my best friends."

"Thanks for saying that, Sarah. You're my best friend, too. I know the Lord brought us together to help each other. That's why I need to talk with you now. Something has been on my mind and has been troubling me for many years. I'm becom-ing more depressed, and I pray for help, but the answers never seem to come. I'm trying my best to do what's right and to be happy, but I feel like I'm stuck, and not progressing. I've been called to help with planning activities for my Relief Society group at church, but that doesn't involve me as much as I need. I feel more isolated. I remember what Trisha taught me about Christlike love. Thinking about that has really been the only thing that keeps me going."

"I understand some of what you're telling me, Ruth, but I can see that something is weighing down heavily on you. You mentioned that a troubling issue has been on your mind, and that you feel like the Lord hasn't been blessing you as much as He has blessed me. Is it something to do with not having your own family?"

"Sarah, you surely have the Spirit with you. It has much to do with that. I told you some years ago that I lost my husband a while back, and didn't have any children with him. You helped cheer me up then when I felt like I was a failure in life. Well, there's more to it than that. Sarah, I really need your help now." Ruth's voice is trembling now.

"Ruth, how can I help you? I'm here for you. I'm willing to give you the emotional support you need."

"You're a very kind person, Sarah. I need to tell you something important that I've never told anyone before. I need to get it out of me as I seek your assistance. I need to tell you what happened to me." She pauses momentarily while looking at Sarah. "I'm a very tender person, and I've had some intense trauma in my life. But, before I talk about that, I first need to explain that I'm a convert to the Church. When I was a junior in high school, there were a couple of girls in my music class who were very good friends of mine. They could see that I was not very happy each day when they were around me. They told me that they are members of this particular Church, where they have information about how to receive more beneficial blessings in their lives, which helps them feel happier each day. They encouraged me to listen to this information, as they felt it would help me feel better.

"I did, along with my sister, Esther. My two friends met with us, along with two missionaries they had contacted. We both felt something very emotional, something that I really felt was missing in my life. When they finished teaching us, we both felt that we should be baptized into the Church. My parents were unhappy with us doing this, but they allowed us to be baptized anyway. They thought that nothing would really come from it. However, after my baptism and confirmation, I had such a very special feeling throughout my whole being. I knew for certain it was right.

"During my teenage years, I loved to sing. I enjoyed singing in the choir of my parents' religion. I always felt a spiritual sensation when I did this, which made me feel happy. I even sang in a special Christmas choir for our community when I was only twelve. I felt so special and happy doing that, but it always seemed like there was something missing. After I joined the Church, and attended the meetings, I felt more complete. I felt that the rest of my life would be so wonderful. I felt that after I graduated high school, I could meet the right person to marry and raise a good family in the Church.

"At age twenty, I met and married a person who seemed very nice. His roots were from Africa as well. He was courteous at first, like Randy was with you. But then, his kindness started decreasing. We were planning on having a good family, but nothing happened. My doctor checked me, and we found out that I'm not able to have children." Ruth's face shows some sad emotion. "He felt it was very unlikely that my condition could ever change. Sarah, I felt so devastated. When my husband was told all this, he became more aggressive and told me that he had married the wrong person. This devastated me even further." Tears begin forming in her eyes. "He started being more violent with me, hitting me, so I had to hide to keep myself from being injured worse. I called the domestic abuse hotline. The authorities came and were able to remove him, and the officers put a restraining order on him. We had to file for divorce. I then felt so worthless." Ruth puts her head down and starts crying.

Sarah takes Ruth's hand and tenderly says, "Ruth, I'm here for you." She pauses for a moment, and then continues with, "I'll keep this confidential between us. You should finish what you're telling me. I feel that it will help you to get it all out."

Ruth looks up with wet eyes and face. Sarah hands her some tissues. After wiping her face, Ruth then continues with great emotion. "Sarah, I found out later ... I found out later, not very long after the divorce was final, that ... my ex-husband ... had killed himself." Ruth starts crying uncontrollably. Sarah gets up and puts her arms around her.

"It's okay, Ruth," Sarah comfortingly says. "I strongly feel your emotions. It's okay to let them out. Your feelings are very important. I'll listen as long as you need."

After a few moments, Ruth looks up and takes Sarah's hand. She explains between sobs, "Sarah, I feel like I'm such a failure. I can't have kids, and the only person who ever wanted to be my husband, killed himself because of it." She sobs more, then continues. "My doctor then told me I needed to have a hysterectomy. This really devastated me when I had to go have it done." She cries some more, then continues between sobs, "Sarah, I'm a real person, a very real person. People don't seem to realize that. Many people were staying away from me, probably because of who I am. I wasn't comfortable going to church.

"All I had was my sister, Esther, who talked with me on the phone. She helped me find part-time work, to help pay for my subsidized housing. I loved to read books when I was at home. Sarah, this has been my life as an adult. After some years had passed, my housing terminated, and I had to move. I asked the Lord in prayer what to do. My sister told me about some reasonable apartments where you were living, and I felt impressed to rent the one where I am now living. My sister is helping me with the rent. I had a part-time job for a little while, which then ended, so our Church leader said he would assist me with some of my food, when I go to church and obey the commandments. He found a few people in the community I could do work for, to earn some money. I love helping people.

"When I started attending church there, I remember you came up to me and welcomed me. You put your arms around me. I felt so, so happy and excited that someone actually cared about me. You told me about your children, and the third on the way. I felt so useful when you told me I could help you. You've literally been a lifesaver for me." Ruth sheds some more tears.

Sarah gently responds with, "Thank you. You've definitely

been through some difficult times in your life. We all have trials, and I really feel for you. I know you have very tender feelings. I know you don't understand why you haven't been able to have your own family, when you see so many successful families. You know I've had my trials, too, like when Randy left me. You were such a comfort to me, more than you realize. You lovingly helped me and my children get through that time. I sincerely appreciate your doing that. You were there when Trish wasn't able to go to school anymore. That meant a whole lot to me."

Ruth starts to smile slightly, and says, "Sarah, that truly was the turning point in my life. Trisha taught me more about Christlike love than I had ever known before. I really understood then how to love other people the way that Christ does. Sarah, you have such a wonderful family. You now have a good husband, you have a returned missionary who is very upright, and you have a successful daughter who knows what she's doing in life. However, I still feel stuck much of the time. Knowing you and your family, and the friendship you all have for me, I feel more hope for myself. But I don't know the Lord's plan for me. Why do I have to experience all these trials, challenges, and hardships in my life? Why can't I have a family of my own? What's going to happen to me?"

Sarah looks very tenderly at Ruth's longing face. She lovingly explains, "Ruth, I know you desperately desire to fit in with other people, and feel like you belong. I understand. Ethan went through many of the same emotions as he was growing up, having Asperger's. He struggled, and I could see the hurt he carried for many years. When we met with Robert, I understood much more about the Lord's plan for each person. Ruth, our Savior is very aware of what you're experiencing in life. He knows your feelings and emotions in detail. He tenderly feels your periods of crying when you're alone at home. Through His atonement, He has literally experienced *everything* which you experience in your life. He loves you very much, as I do, and wants you to feel happy in life.

"Ruth, I definitely know that our Savior has His specific plan for you, a very wonderful plan. He knows you don't have a family. Everything you have experienced and are experiencing is actually for your good. You are learning things you couldn't learn any other way. He has lovingly laid everything out for you, so that you can progress in the best possible manner. Ruth, you are a very tender, spiritual person. Our Savior knows who you are, and knows you by name. As you stay faithful and as you earnestly pour out your heart to our Heavenly Father, telling Him about your feelings and the very longings of your heart, and sincerely desiring His help and support, you will receive blessings in addition to what you now have, to help you during your struggles. You have friends who help you, and you have your sister who cares about you. She also brought you a loving kitty cat, so that you would not feel so lonely.

"As you are faithful, our Savior will help you, and your burdens will be lighter. Then, you have the glorious promise that you will receive a wonderful, loving husband, whether in this life or the next, and later you will have a very loving eternal family, all sealed to you, which will bring you indescribable joy. They will continue blessing your life forever. This is the promise of forever families. Ruth, I certainly know this, as well as I see you sitting here by me right now."

"That's so wonderful to hear. Sarah, I've always felt your strong spirit, and your great amount of love. You're a real lifesaver for me. I couldn't have asked for a better friend." Ruth lowers her head a little and starts showing some tears of joy. Sarah stands up and gives her a big hug. Ruth then continues with an emotional voice, "I feel the Lord's Spirit with you, telling me that what you're saying is true, that I will have a wonderful family, who will always bring me great joy. I can hardly wait! Thank you so much for your kind words to me."

Sarah then peacefully explains, "Remember, we will all have more trials to experience in this life, through our Lord's plan, but also remember that He will help us and He will bless us as we experience more challenges." Sarah takes her hand and says, "I have a great amount of love for you, like Christ has for you. I know you'll make it."

Standing up, Ruth gratefully responds, "I can feel that coming from you. I can feel it, just like I felt it with Trisha." Her face again shows a joyful expression, and she says, "I feel that Trisha is here with us right now, comforting me like she did before, and showing her great love for me. She's such a wonderful person, just like you."

"Thank you, Ruth. You're a very kind, sweet person. Our Savior definitely brought us together, so that we can help and edify each other. This is part of His loving plan for us. Let's go see if Lexi is back yet. When she's back home, we can lovingly offer our assistance, just like Christ would. Being more like Him in all we do, and showing our love toward others will definitely bring more happiness in our lives."

They both dry their eyes before leaving the room. Ruth is joyfully beaming, as she feels the great weight that's been pressing heavily on her is now lifted, and is completely gone.

They find Wayne and Ethan happily working together on their wood figurine projects. Wayne is teaching Ethan some of the fine arts of woodworking, which he enjoys learning. They notice that Ruth is looking much happier.

Ethan says, "Ruth, you look wonderful. I'm happy for you. You appear like the families I taught the gospel on my mission, just after they were baptized. I can see the Spirit with you. Mom, you're always so good at helping people."

They both respond to Ethan with gratitude. Wayne then says, "It's so good everyone's happy. I can hardly wait for lunch. Is Lexi home yet? She makes such good meals. It's like eating at a luxury restaurant. It's so delicious."

"We are going to check," says Sarah. "If she isn't here yet, she should be soon."

They wait, while doing some items around the house. It's

closer to lunchtime now, and she hasn't arrived yet. Sarah tries calling her on her phone, with no result. They're becoming concerned, so Sarah says, "I'll take Ruth with me, and we'll see if we can find her."

They get into Sarah's vehicle and travel toward the downtown area. Sarah sees the road partially blocked ahead by a couple of police cars and a fire engine, with their emergency lights flashing. These vehicles are surrounding another car and a motorcycle lying in the traffic lane. She merges over to the left to get through and to see what's happening. Sarah suddenly lets out a gasp and exclaims, "That's Lexi's car! I hope she's okay!"

She stops her vehicle on the side of the street a little bit ahead of the scene, and she and Ruth immediately walk toward the area, until an officer putting up tape stops them. He tells them, "You two cannot go any further until we finish our investigation into this serious accident scene."

Sarah quickly responds, "It looks like that person over there is my daughter. I know her car."

"Okay, come with me."

They go with the officer and find out that indeed, Alexis is the person in the car. She is unharmed, but she is very emotional. Another officer is talking with her. A motorcyclist had apparently turned in front of her, and she wasn't able to stop in time. An ambulance has arrived, and the paramedics are loading the man into the ambulance. Alexis' car has some minor-to-moderate frontal-end damage, but is drivable.

The two officers meet and begin conversing. Sarah quickly goes up to her and asks, "Lexi, Lexi, are you alright? I'm sorry this had to happen to you. Are you hurt at all?"

Alexis looks at her mother and responds with much emotion, as more tears form in her eyes. "Oh, Mom. I feel so bad. I just couldn't stop in time. I hope he's okay." She lets out a couple of sobs.

"Lexi, it's okay. They'll take good care of him. Our Savior is certainly watching out for you. We'll help you bring the food home."

"Thanks, Mom. It's so good you're here at a time like this. I feel better now. The policeman said he's finished talking with me. I still want to make our special lunch."

"Okay, let's all carry the food to my car, and Ruth will take you home. I'll stay here and bring your car back when they allow me. You're alright, Lexi."

They load the food into Sarah's car. Sarah gives Alexis a hug, and Ruth drives her home. On the way, Alexis apologetically says, "Ruth, I feel so bad. I thought I could take a shortcut home so I could get an earlier start on lunch. I guess I turned onto the wrong street, and was trying to get back on the right street again when this happened. I know I should've done better. I'm so sorry."

"Don't worry about it, Lexi," Ruth says in response. "Things happen, but they're for our good. The Lord has His special plan for you. You're doing just fine."

"Ruth, I notice you're much happier now than you were earlier. I can see you feel much better about life."

"I sure do. Lexi, your mom certainly is a wonderful person. She's very helpful and has a lot of love to give. You're so blessed to have her as your mother."

"Thanks, Ruth. She's helped all of us kids, especially Ethan. She just has a way of saying the right things to help us feel better. I can frequently feel the Spirit with her."

"That's certainly true. Well, it looks like we're almost home. I can hardly wait for your lunch. It's like eating at a gourmet restaurant."

Alexis lowers her head a little, and quietly and humbly responds, "Thank you very much. I try."

"Well, for me, you're the best chef in the world. You'll do very well. I'll help you carry the food in, and I'll be here for anything else you need."

"Thank you. You're a very special friend, and I sincerely

wish the best for you."

Ruth is grateful for Alexis' sincerity. They arrive home, and Ruth helps carry in the groceries. She tells Wayne and Ethan about what has happened, and they're both very grateful that Alexis is okay. They eagerly await Sarah's return. She soon comes home, and they all enjoy a wonderful, delicious lunch.

The motorcyclist recovers well from his serious injuries, and his insurance, along with the coverage which Alexis has, completely covers the cost of repairs to her car. The repairs are completed in time for her return to school and work. During this time, everyone enjoys visiting together and enjoying some great, tasty meals, compliments of Alexis. When it's time for her to go back to her own place at the university, everyone gives her a hug. They compliment her on her great talent, and wish her a safe trip back. She smiles and waves as she leaves.

Chapter Six

A WONDERFUL NEIGHBOR

T HE new week begins and the time comes for Sarah and Ethan to return to their work, so they both take Ruth back to her place. They first plan to visit her neighbor, the Loveless family, who bought their former house. They arrive, and all three go to their front door.

Lisa Loveless, the wife and mother, opens the door. She recognizes Ruth and invites them inside. They go in, and Lisa invites them to have a seat in the living room. Ruth introduces Sarah and Ethan to her. She says, "Lisa, these are my good neighbors who lived here before you moved in. Ethan is Sarah's son. We helped each other so well. It was sad to see them go."

Lisa then says to Sarah, "Ruth has told me so much about you. I'm very impressed that Ruth has been able to help you so well. Knowing this, we wanted to move here and get to know her better. We already know her sister, Esther, who has been very kind to us. Ruth is such a great friend, and we all go to church together. My husband, Matt, and my three teenage daughters like her as well." She looks at Ruth, who is smiling.

"My daughters especially enjoy her friendship. As you know, they're busy with their own lives and friends at school, but we get together at times on Sundays and enjoy her company."

Sarah responds, "That's good to hear. Ruth surely is a very wonderful person. She's helped me in so many ways. She's very willing to help you, too, when you have a need. She loves to help people. Is anyone else home for us to meet?"

"No, Matt is at work, and my daughters aren't home right now. Some other time when you're this way, you can meet them."

"Sounds good. Well, Ethan, we need to go to work now and check out how things are going there. It's been great meeting you, Lisa. I'd love to meet the rest of your family soon."

As everyone stands, Ethan looks at Lisa and says, "It's also good to meet you and get to know you. I wish the best for you and your family."

"Thank you, Ethan. I can tell you're a very spiritual person, like your mother. Are you a returned missionary?"

"Yes, I am. I enjoyed serving a successful mission in Argentina for two years. It was very good for me."

"So, you speak Spanish. My two oldest daughters are learning Spanish in school, and Matt served a Spanish-speaking mission in Peru. I'd like to get to know you more, and you can share some conversation in Spanish. My daughters want to learn to speak it better. Maybe we can all plan a time to have dinner together," Lisa says as she looks at Sarah.

"That sounds like a great plan," responds Sarah.

"Okay, we'll plan on it. It was fun meeting both of you."

"Ethan and I need to leave now. What about you, Ruth?"

She replies, "If it's okay with you, Lisa, is it fine if I stay a little longer?"

"That'll be great. I happen to have some free time right now, so Ruth and I can visit some more. I see that she would enjoy that," Lisa responds while turning toward Sarah.

"Okay," Sarah says. "We'll see you both later." She gives

Ruth a hug, and they both leave. As it's not quite midmorning yet, they go to the consulting company building to take care of some items there. Ruth stays and shares many of her recent experiences with Lisa. Ruth tells her how she feels more encouraged, and explains that she would like to help them wherever possible. Lisa is very appreciative of her willingness to help. She now notices more of a glow about Ruth.

They chat for quite a while. Lisa invites Ruth to have a quick lunch together, then the two younger girls come home. They're both excited to see Ruth there, and join in the conversation. They tell her about the exciting activities they've been involved in at school and with their friends. Both of them also notice that Ruth now seems happier. They ask their mother if Ruth can stay for dinner. She tells them that it's up to Ruth, who graciously accepts. Ruth is excited that her neighbor family is now friendlier with her.

Later, the oldest daughter arrives, then Matt comes home. They're happy to see Ruth there and plan to enjoy a wonderful dinner and evening together. They all notice that she's more talkative now, and they really enjoy her company. Afterward, Lisa takes her to her own place, saying that she will call her more often and have her come and assist when needed, as well as visit. When Lisa arrives back home, she tells her husband about the change she has noticed in Ruth. Matt has also noticed it. He explains that it is more enjoyable to have her at their house, now that she is more positive with herself and with life.

A few days later, Lisa calls Ruth and asks if she can come over to help. She explains that her youngest daughter is quite sick, and needs to stay home from school. Lisa also tells her about her need to run several errands, as well as needing to fulfill some other obligations she had planned that day. She explains that her youngest, Jaclyn, isn't comfortable staying home by herself, and isn't really able to get her own lunch, in her present condition.

Ruth says that she will be right over, and is glad to help. She enjoys being with Jaclyn as well. She goes over to their house, and Lisa gives her the needed information, gives her a hug of appreciation, then leaves. Jaclyn has already been told that Ruth will be there with her. Ruth goes up to her bedroom, and on the way, she has a flashback of when she was helping Trisha in the very same house, in the very same bedroom. She remembers the Christlike love which Trisha showed to her and taught her, which makes her feel very emotional. She really feels the Lord's Spirit with her.

Having had this flashback, Ruth feels renewed energy and love as she goes in to check on Jaclyn. She knocks, then enters with a smile and says, "Hi, Jacs. I'm here to help you today. Do you need anything now?"

She responds, "Yeah. Please bring me some more juice. It's really good, and it helps me feel better."

"Alright then. Anything else you need?"

"Not right now. I feel like sleeping a little more. Later, when we have lunch, maybe you could help me with some of my school assignment. There's a part that I don't understand very well."

"Okay, Jacs. I'll try to help where I can. I'll let you know when it's about time for lunch. I'll be as quiet as possible, so you can sleep." (Jacs is a nickname Ruth calls her, and has many times earlier. She loves this nickname as a fourteen-year-old.)

Ruth brings her the juice, then goes back down to the living room. As Jaclyn takes a nap, Ruth reads some inspirational Church messages she brought with her. Sarah had suggested that she do this more, as it especially brings the Lord's Spirit into the person's life in great abundance. As she does this, she realizes that Sarah's words to her are very true. She begins to feel more hope in her life, and she has more of a desire to help other people be happier.

She becomes rather involved with the inspirational messages, and loses track of the time. She suddenly realizes that it's time to prepare lunch for the two of them. She happily goes to the kitchen, with which she's very familiar. She has another flashback of times when she was there with the Wilkinson family, and Alexis had prepared some very excellent meals for everyone. She emotionally thinks about the times she prepared lunch for Trisha in that same kitchen. She remembers the loving memories of the happy times she experienced there. Ruth becomes a bit more emotional as she ponders this, along with what she has just read. She feels extremely joyful as she prepares a good lunch for both of them.

When lunch is ready, the aroma of the tasty food awakens Jaclyn, and she calls down, "Ruth, is that our lunch? It sure smells good. Is that your cooking?"

"It sure is, Jacs. I'll bring some up to you in a minute."

"It smells so good, even with my cold. I want you to eat with me. It'll be fun to have you here when we eat our lunch."

"Okay, I'll be right up."

Ruth takes up Jaclyn's tray, then her own. She has a special recipe she uses for sandwiches and soup. Lisa has some excellent ingredients, and the combination results in a very good lunch.

Jaclyn exclaims, "Wow! This is good! I didn't know you could cook *this* well. Maybe we could all have dinner together again soon, when I'm well, and you can make this great soup for everyone."

Ruth is very happy with Jaclyn's comment, and cheerfully responds, "Thanks so much, Jacs. I didn't know I made it that good, but I'm happy you're really enjoying it."

"Eating this is helping me feel better already. Thanks for being here today with me."

They finish their lunch together, and Ruth cleans up. She then helps Jaclyn on her school assignment, and it turns out that Ruth is quite knowledgeable in that particular subject of world geography. Jaclyn is very excited that she is able to help her so well. She stays and chats with her for a bit, then Jaclyn needs to sleep again for a while.

Ruth is in the living room when Lisa comes home. Ruth tells her that all went well and that they had a good time together. She thanks Ruth, who then leaves. Lisa goes up to see Jaclyn, who is working some more on her assignment.

She excitedly tells her mom, "It was so fun with Ruth here today. Guess what? Ruth makes the best soup in the world! I want her back here to make it for all of us, okay?"

"You liked it that much? Well, I can ask her and see if she would like to do it. You really enjoy being with Ruth. That's wonderful. She appears so much happier now. We can have her back again soon."

"That'll be so fun."

The following Sunday evening, Lisa invites Ruth to come for dinner, and asks her if she would like to make her soup again. She is delighted to come and do this. Jaclyn has mostly recovered from her illness, and is enjoying their great dinner together with Ruth. The Loveless family is even greater friends with her, and she feels better with them, as well. Ruth is very thankful for them, and even more thankful for the assistance which Sarah gave her, to help her understand how to be happier around everyone and enjoy life. She sees how being more loving toward others has made a difference in her relationship with people. She now feels much better about her life.

Ruth has spoken highly about Sarah and Ethan to Lisa, who is excited to meet them again. The next Sunday evening, Lisa invites all three of them to come and visit for a while, along with Wayne, and to have him, Sarah, and Ethan meet her entire family. They come with Ruth, and they shake hands with all the family. Lisa has already told her husband and her two oldest daughters about Ethan's mission in Argentina, so after they are all comfortably seated in the living room, Matt asks Ethan to tell them more about his mission experiences.

Ethan shares some very spiritual and touching moments he had while teaching the people there. The entire family feels touched by the emotional experiences he is sharing. Matt then shares some of his experiences he had during his mission in Peru. He then asks Ethan some other questions about his mission in Spanish, to which Ethan replies very well. The two oldest daughters are intently listening as they are conversing. They can understand some of their conversation, especially the oldest. However, Wayne, Sarah, and Ruth cannot understand them, but are enjoying watching their expressions.

The oldest daughter then asks Ethan to explain some information she doesn't understand, that has been confusing to her, which her Spanish teacher was presenting in her class during the past week. He answers her questions in an easy-to-understand manner, which makes her very happy. She is able to comfortably complete her assignment, and is excited to do it, as she now comprehends it much easier. She then sincerely expresses her gratitude to him. Ethan wishes the two of them well in their Spanish classes.

Lisa invites everyone to stay for dinner, which she has left cooking while they've been talking. They graciously accept, and everybody goes into the dining room when it's ready. Matt says a prayer and blessing on their food, and they converse about various subjects, including Spanish while they're eating. The subject comes up about members of the Church who have various disorders, and the entire Loveless family is extremely shocked when Ethan tells them that he was diagnosed on the autism spectrum.

Lisa remarks, "Ethan, I had absolutely no idea that you are autistic! You appear as you don't have any disorder. Who would have known? Wow, this is amazing!"

He responds, "I've had my difficulties, though. It was hard for me when I was in school, but then we met with this wonderful person who also has Asperger's, and who has completely overcome it. He taught me how to do the same with the Lord's help, and it was a miracle. I have been able to fulfill the Lord's plan for me already, and I know I'll be able to do much more with His help."

"Well, this truly is amazing, what you've been able to accomplish so far. You served a two-year mission in Argentina, and you now have good employment. I'm learning so much more about how our Savior is able to bless people in ways I never knew. Matt, what do you think of all this?"

"I agree with you, Lisa. Our Savior does greatly bless people. Ethan, I'll always remember this evening getting acquainted with you. I can just feel your spirituality."

"Thank you, Matt," Ethan responds. "It's been wonderful getting to know you and your great family also. I can really feel your spirituality here in your home."

"Thanks for the compliment. It's also been good meeting both of you, Wayne and Sarah, and learning more about you. I can tell you are all a very good family."

Sarah shows her appreciation for their compliments, and for the dinner and their hospitality throughout the evening. Wayne, Ethan, and Ruth then do the same. They visit together for quite a while, getting to know each other more. As the time is growing late, they say their goodbyes and are ready to leave. Jaclyn then goes up to Ruth, wanting her to stay longer. Ruth feels very happy at this request, but tells her that she has to go now, and that she will be able to return soon. Ruth then gives her a big hug. Jaclyn feels okay with this, and kindly says her goodbyes. The four then leave, being very grateful for having met such a great family, Ruth's wonderful neighbor.

Chapter Seven

FAITH DURING A SEVERE TRIAL

RUTH is enjoying her association with the Loveless family, along with some other members of her Church ward. Sarah and Ethan also stop in at times to see her and to visit and find out how she's doing. She tells them that she has been feeling better, and is enjoying talking with more people.

During one of their visits with her, she tells Sarah that her financial situation isn't so good now, and that she's not sure how things are going to improve for her. She tells both of them that her sister isn't able to help her much, financially, and that she is receiving some food assistance. Ruth is very concerned about her situation, and has been praying about it. She asks Sarah what she should do.

Sarah excitedly responds with, "Ruth, I have good news, and I believe we're the answer to your prayers. As you know, I'm a director and supervisor/manager of the phone and internet consulting company where I work, along with Ethan here. There's an opening coming available, as one of my workers is leaving. Before coming today, I received this very strong prompting that you should be the one to fill that position. How does that sound?"

"Oh, Sarah, that's such wonderful news," Ruth responds with much emotion. "This will be so wonderful, working with you. I really feel that our Savior is helping me."

"It will be great having you with us. It pays well, and you will be working full-time. You'll also have excellent benefits, including complete health insurance and paid leave, which includes all major holidays. I believe this is just what you need."

"Oh, thank you, thank you. I feel so happy now; I feel so blessed." Ruth sheds some tears of joy.

Ethan then comments, "It'll be fun having you work with us, too. It's really great work, and I know you'll enjoy it. We can teach you; it's quite easy to learn."

Sarah then tells her, "We will come and get you each morning and bring you back each evening, Monday through Friday. We would love to help you this way."

"This is so wonderful. I really, truly feel this is right for me. Thanks for considering me." She is showing a great amount of happiness.

"Alright then, be ready at 7:45 Monday morning, and we'll be here. It'll be great having you on our team! There will be some paperwork to fill out when you begin, and we'll help you through the first day. I'm sure you'll pick it up quickly."

"Thanks so much. Sarah, you're a real lifesaver."

They talk some more before Sarah and Ethan leave. Ruth feels very joyful all that evening, and sleeps well that night.

Monday morning comes and she is ready when they arrive. They all go to the phone and internet consulting building and Sarah gives her the initial orientation, along with the paperwork for a new full-time employee. Ruth understands the orientation very well, and Sarah is available to answer any questions. She then has Ethan work close by her throughout the day to assist with the various procedures. She picks it up rather quickly, and is very pleased with herself. She's excited to do this work to help other people, as well as to receive a good income now. She's also pleased to have excellent health insurance coverage.

The next few weeks go very well for Ruth. She is enjoying her work, and is becoming very proficient at it. Sarah tells her that at this rate, she could easily become a group leader in the near future, which would include a small increase in pay, in addition to regular raises. Ruth is very happy to hear this, as she feels that she can easily assist the other workers in her group. Ethan has already become a group leader in his group, and is happy doing it.

Partway through the following month, Ruth notices that she is feeling weaker and more tired. She feels that something isn't right, so Sarah takes her to her doctor during their lunch break for a checkup, along with various health screenings. She is past middle-age now, and her doctor feels that these screenings are more important to keep current. She is scheduled to go back for two important screenings: colon and breast. After these are completed, she has a follow-up visit with her doctor. Arranging leave from work, she takes the bus. When her doctor comes in, he informs her that the screenings and blood level and blood work checks are all mostly fine, except for one major discovery. He says that she has stage-two breast cancer, and it is rapidly progressing to nearly stage three.

Ruth is devastated and exclaims, "Oh no! I don't need this! Why is this happening to me? Why? Things have been going so well. I can't have this now!"

Her doctor responds, "Ruth, we need to start chemo and radiation treatment on you immediately, and see how it goes. There's a good chance that you'll respond well. If not, then surgery may be needed."

Ruth puts her head down and moans, "No, no, I don't want this. Lord, why are you doing this to me? I've been so blessed, and now I can't even go to work. I feel so terrible."

Her doctor then says to her, "I know this is something that many people find difficult to hear, but as I said, there's a good chance that you will go into remission. I'll set you up to be admitted to the hospital tomorrow morning, and we can get started. This will be the best way to take care of it. I know it will be inconvenient, but the sooner we start, the better off you'll be. We don't want it to become metastatic."

"Okay, I guess so. I'll need to call Sarah to come and get me, and let her know what's happening, that I can't go to work right now. Oh, how I wish this wasn't happening to me. I don't want this to be true." Ruth looks down, her hands shake, and her eyes fill with tears.

The doctor gives her the information for the hospital, and her check-in time. She calls Sarah to come get her at the clinic and bring her back to work.

When she arrives, Ruth sobbingly tells her, "Sarah, I have some very bad news." She puts her head down and begins to cry.

Sarah asks, "Ruth, what is it? What's wrong?"

Ruth barely mumbles the words, "I ... have ... breast cancer."

"Oh no. Ruth, I really feel for you. How bad is it?" Sarah puts her hand on Ruth's shoulder.

Through her tears, she responds, "My doctor says it's stage two, and progressing rapidly. He says I need to be at the hospital tomorrow morning for chemo, and that it should help me. Sarah, I can't believe this is happening to me." Ruth puts her head down again.

"I can't believe it, either. This is such a shock to hear. I know you want to be at work. I'll make arrangements there for your absence. The good thing is, you'll receive your pay for much of your leave. Ruth, things will work out. I'll earnestly pray for you, that you'll quickly go into remission. I'm here to help you."

"Thank you so much. You're such a special person for saying that. You're helping me feel a little better already."

"Ruth, I really care about you. You can take it easy the rest of the day, and I'll get you tomorrow morning and get you settled at the hospital. Things will be okay."

Sarah takes her back to the workplace to rest. She explains to Ethan what is happening, who is very concerned. He wishes her a speedy recovery. As Ruth needs to take a leave of absence, Sarah's bookkeeper fills in for Ruth, and Ethan includes the bookkeeping responsibilities with his own work. As Ethan is excellent at math, accounting comes very naturally to him.

After the workday is over, Ethan suggests to Sarah and Ruth that he give Ruth a blessing. Ruth is very willing to have this, so after everyone leaves, they go into Sarah's office and Ethan gives her an excellent, spiritual blessing, where she is promised that all will work out well for her as she stays close to the Lord, and that this trial is for her experience and growth. She's blessed that her suffering will be lessened. Ruth feels much hope afterward, and feels the Lord's Spirit very strongly. She thanks Ethan for the wonderful blessing. They take her home, and Sarah explains that she'll be there early in the morning, and wishes her a good sleep that night.

The next morning, Sarah and Ethan arrive to take Ruth to the hospital before their work begins. She feels very tired, but is able to be ready on time. They take her and get her checked in, and they help her with the paperwork which includes her excellent health insurance coverage. Sarah gives her a hug and wishes her well, and Ethan promises that she'll be okay. This helps Ruth feel more comforted. They both then leave for work.

Ruth is taken in for some detailed verification scans and tests. She's given a couple of medications, then they begin the chemotherapy and other treatment. The next day she starts to feel very nauseous, and asks the nurse for more of the medication to help her feel more comfortable. It helps a little, but she is still experiencing much discomfort. She then remembers the blessing that Ethan gave her. Thinking of this helps her to feel a little better. She remembers Ethan saying that Christ has already felt all her suffering, and that she won't suffer as much when she puts her heartfelt faith and trust in Christ, and as she prays to receive the comfort she needs.

Ruth is alone in her hospital room, feeling very sick and needing physical and emotional comfort. She begins to earnestly pray to Heavenly Father for comfort from her misery. During her individual prayer, she has the sweet flashback of the time when she was preparing lunch for herself and Trisha. Ruth thinks about what Trisha told her about Christ's atoning sacrifice, about how much love He has for us, so that we can become as He is, and have forever families. She thinks about what Sarah told her concerning her ability to later have a sweet, forever family of her own. She immediately feels a peaceful warmth travel throughout her body, and her discomfort decreases right then. She continues to pray, thanking God for the rapid answer to her prayer. She prays that she will be able to sleep well, and that she will be able to handle her discomfort with His help. Ruth intensely feels Christ's love and peace with her, which helps her feel hope that she will get better.

After a week in the hospital, her first radiation treatment is finished, which the doctor had ordered for her, and she is allowed to go home to recover. At the beginning of all this, Ruth had called her sister, Esther, to tell her about her cancer, who was very sympathetic about it. She explained that she could come and stay with Ruth, and help take care of her needs. At the time of being released from the hospital, Esther comes and takes her home. She really desires that Ruth is able to quickly recover, and go into remission. She follows the doctor's orders exactly, in giving her the medications, along with all the other instructions she was given. This helps Ruth to feel more comfortable and increases the chance of remission.

All this is causing Ruth to lose her beautiful, shiny black hair, which saddens her. The next evening, she is feeling very depressed, and complains to Esther, "I'm so sad that my lovely hair is coming out, and is almost gone. I don't want anyone to see me like this. Why does this have to happen? Why do I have to go through all this?"

Esther, who is a faithful member of the Church, tenderly responds, "Ruth, trials happen to everyone. This is part of life. Remember, you have many blessings, and you have me to help you. My good friends, the Loveless family, have welcomed you, and it's great they live so close. You've told me about your friend, Sarah, who has helped you so much. You're so blessed to have her in your life. Ruth, I know you hate losing your hair. If you want, I could help you with obtaining a good wig to wear. Would you like that?"

"Esther, I don't know. If it looks right, maybe so. I just don't feel very happy right now. This is so hard for me." Ruth is showing more sadness.

"Ruth, let's have a prayer together. I definitely know that will help you feel better. How about it?"

"Okay, it sounds good to me."

Esther says a very spiritual prayer, asking for the Lord's help for her sister, and that she will have a good outcome. She asks that Ruth will be comfortable and feel the Lord's Spirit with her to help comfort her. She thanks God for all their blessings, asking that He will grant them those blessings which they need. Ruth feels better afterward, and gives her sister a big hug.

Ruth goes to the hospital four more times in the following weeks for more rounds of chemotherapy and radiation treatment, along with appointments for additional radiation treatments. The chemo causes her a great amount of discomfort, but her sister is frequently right by her to comfort her. Ruth wishes that her chemo treatment wouldn't be so intense; however, she endures it well through prayer and through her sister's assistance. Esther finds a particular wig to Ruth's liking, which she uses when she's around people.

On one of these occasions when Ruth is home with her

sister, Sarah and Ethan stop by after work. They have come to check how she's doing.

After entering and greeting Esther, Sarah says, "Ruth, it's so good to see you. You're looking well. I'm so happy your sister, Esther, is here to help. How's the treatment going for you?"

"It's going okay, I guess. It sure is so uncomfortable. I don't ever want to go through this again. My doctor says I'm improving, but he will have to wait and see how it goes. It's going to take a while. I just hope it will go away quickly."

"Yes, I do too. It's hard to see you go through all this, having been close friends for these many years." Sarah takes Ruth's hand and continues. "Ruth, I know the Lord is greatly blessing you, and I strongly feel that you'll be better again. I have this feeling that our Lord has more great work for you to do on this Earth."

Ruth feels a bit emotional, and responds, "Sarah, you're such a good friend. I know we'll be friends forever. I'm just so happy that our Savior guided me to you those many years ago. I frequently feel His great love for me, especially now. Again, that was impressed on me so much when I had that wonderful experience with Trisha. I'll never forget that feeling I felt after she told me about Christ's atonement, and looked at me so lovingly. I felt her love, and Christ's love and Spirit so strongly. I knew it was a tender mercy from our Savior. I just know so much more about Christ and His love for me."

Ethan has been listening to all these tender comments coming from Ruth. He then lovingly says, "I know for sure everything you're saying is definitely true. Our Savior loves you tremendously, and has His very, very important plan for you. I know you need to go through this trial now for your experience and for your good. Christ is preparing you for greater, more wonderful experiences in the future. He knows what a choice person you are, and He's lovingly helping you develop more faith and trust in His plan for you, so that you'll know with even more surety that He's real, and that He has tremendous blessings for you.

"Ruth, I feel you'll be an extremely loving mother after this life, and that many people will look up to you for guidance in their lives. You'll be a wonderful example to them. I know you'll have tremendous joy during that time. You remember I mentioned all this in my priesthood blessing I gave you. I also know Christ has His important mission for you on this Earth, that you'll be helping other people feel happier, as I have."

Ruth tearfully responds, "I feel the Spirit so strongly here, telling me that what you've said is all true. I really feel it is, and that the Lord wants to help me and bless me. Wow, it's great to know that our Savior has such a great plan for me. It's such a marvelous thing. You, and your sister and mother, including Trisha are very spiritual people. You're all such wonderful friends to me. Thank you so much."

Esther is sitting next to Ruth, who also has tears in her eyes. She stands up and gives Ethan and Sarah a big hug, and says, "Ruth is right. I feel my Savior's love for me as well, that He also has His special plan for me. It's so wonderful, knowing all this." She then gives her sister a great big hug.

Sarah and Ethan stay and talk with them for a while longer; Sarah then announces that they need to leave to go home, and prepare dinner for themselves and for Wayne. Ethan shakes hands with them, and Sarah gives them a hug.

Ruth goes back to the hospital one more time for another treatment, along with some more scans and tests. The doctor in charge then announces that Ruth is responding very well, that she's beginning to go into complete remission. This makes Ruth and Esther extremely happy, knowing that the Lord is indeed blessing her. Finishing her stay there, the doctor tells her that no more treatments will be necessary, or any other action, unless the results in the follow-up appointment reveal otherwise. He tells her to continue with her medications, and to continue with a very healthy food diet and plenty of water.

He says she can exercise a little more, to build up her strength, and tells her to keep up the good work, that the worst is behind her.

Ruth and Esther leave, feeling very joyful. When they arrive at Ruth's place, they go inside and kneel at the couch. Ruth then expresses a very sincere, heartfelt prayer of gratitude to Heavenly Father for blessing her so well. She can feel the intense love that He and Christ have for her. She asks Him to bless her with great health now, so that she can do more of His work, in blessing other people. She feels the answer to her prayer, that this will occur. She also asks a blessing on her sister, Esther, that she will receive her needed blessings and comfort. Esther later relates to Ruth that she has felt an increase in her faith as well, that this experience in assisting her sister during this time has also greatly helped her increase her faith in Christ, and to better understand His love for her.

During the follow-up appointment a month later, all tests and scans show that Ruth is in complete remission, which greatly pleases Ruth and Esther. She is told to come back six months later, to verify her continuing remission. They both have a very strong testimony in Christ's power, and in His ability to bless others. Ruth is also very pleased that her beautiful hair is beginning to grow again.

The Loveless family has been visiting her at times throughout her ordeal. They are all very happy that Ruth has recovered so well, especially Lisa and Jaclyn. They didn't want to lose such a great friend. After hearing the news of her complete remission, they invite Ruth and Esther over to have dinner together, and to have a party afterward, to celebrate Ruth's return to good health. This is enjoyed by everyone, and afterward, Ruth and her sister sincerely thank them for their friendship. Ruth then thanks Lisa for taking care of her cat during the times when she was away. Matt and Lisa surely enjoyed this celebration with their good friend, Esther, as well, and they invite her to come visit often, so they can spend more good times together with her and Ruth. Lately, Matt and Lisa have seen even more improvement in Ruth's demeanor, after having experienced this great trial in her life.

89

good times together with her and Ruth. Lately, Matt and Lisa have seen even more improvement in Ruth's demeanor, after having experienced this great trial in her life.

Chapter Eight
LIFE AFTER ASD

ETHAN is doing extremely well, working as a group leader over a number of consultants at his mother's workplace. He has overcome much of his autism disorder, and is continuing his assignment as an accountant, as the worker filling in for Ruth during her absence has left. Ruth is back, working in her position again, and is thoroughly enjoying it. Between her excellent health insurance coverage and great pay, all her medical expenses are paid in full, and she is able to comfortably pay her rent, along with food and her other necessary expenses, and she still has enough to save. She thanks the Lord every day for her blessings.

Esther has now returned back home. Before leaving, Ruth sincerely thanked her for her loving assistance she gave during all this time. Ruth treated her to a special dinner at a fancy restaurant before she left the next morning.

Sarah is successfully working in her routine as manager for the next few weeks at her consulting business with Ethan and Ruth. She's happily working in her office on a particular morning when she suddenly receives an extremely shocking phone call. Alice's brother is calling her to inform her that Alice has just passed away. Sarah is extremely numb at hearing this. She is told to meet him in the office at her care center the next morning, where they will then go and make the arrangements together at the mortuary. He then wishes her a safe trip as she travels to meet him. The call ends, and she just can't believe what she was told only a moment earlier. She puts her head down on her office desk and sobs for a few minutes. After spending a few moments to regain her composure, she slowly gets up and opens her office door. She goes over to Ethan and quietly asks him to come inside the office with her.

He goes in and she closes the door. He's wondering if something is wrong at work, as he notices her sad expression. He asks, "Mom, what's wrong? Is the business okay?"

She has him sit down and sadly says, "Ethan, I just received some sad news on the phone. Alice has passed away."

"Oh, Mom, that's so sad to hear," Ethan responds with great emotion. "I've known her all my life. She's been such a good friend to us. I feel she's very happy now, rejoicing with her family. Mom, she was such a wonderful person, wasn't she."

"She surely was, Ethan," Sarah agrees, while shedding another tear. "We will certainly miss her. I know it's better for her now, not having to deal any more with Alzheimer's."

"I agree. The Lord knows what He's doing. He has His special plan for her, like He has for all of us. It's just that being separated from her in this life is hard, especially right now. I still remember when I was six, when we went to her office, and you told me that's when she diagnosed my Asperger's. I remember putting that fun jigsaw puzzle together. Alice certainly was one of a kind, wasn't she?"

"Yes, she sure was, while she was alive, and she still is. It'll be so great for us, meeting everyone again later, after this life."

"It surely will. It's so wonderful, knowing the Lord's plan for all of us after this life is over."

"Ethan, I know this will be a difficult request, but I need to go to the mortuary, near Alice's care center tomorrow morning. There are some managerial duties which need to be completed during the week, and I know you're very familiar with the procedures here, so I would like you to fill in for me, completing the managerial duties while I'm gone. I can show you the items which need attention. Ethan, I have faith in you."

"Thank you for your faith in me. I understand."

"You're doing very well with your current responsibilities, and you're an excellent bookkeeper, for which I'm very thankful. I know you would like to be at her funeral, but you'll be helping me in a magnificent way. It's good you now have your own car. Things will work out fine for you, and I know the Lord will help you."

"Thank you, again. I feel that I can do this, and that the Lord will help me. I would like to be at her funeral, but I know this is important."

"Ethan, you're a great person. Ruth is doing well in her assignment, along with the other workers. She will be a great help to you. I'll go tell Ruth what's happening, then I'll show you the information you need to know for the next few days. I really appreciate your willingness to do this for me."

"No problem. I'm ready to look at what you need to show me, when you come back in, and I'll do my very best to keep things going well."

"Thanks, Ethan. There are also some reports which need to be completed and sent off as soon as possible. I know your attention to detail, and I feel you'll be able to be a very good manager some day."

"Mom, saying that really means a lot to me. I'll be ready when you come back."

Sarah smiles at him, stands up, and puts her hand on his shoulder as she opens the door and leaves for a minute. Ruth is sad to hear about Alice, but is happy that Ethan will be in charge for the next few days. Sarah then takes care of a couple of issues another group leader is having, then returns and shows Ethan all the pertinent information, and tells him about some other items he needs to know. He then goes back to his work with his group.

Sarah leaves very early the next morning on her five-hour trip to go meet with Alice's brother at the care center. She will be staying in the area for nearly a week, until after the graveside service is completed. Ethan makes his forty-minute drive in his own car to the consulting center, and goes to Sarah's office. He feels very happy with himself, that he's able to do much more now than he previously thought he could. He meets with all the group leaders, and informs them that Sarah will be gone for a few days. He briefs them with the information they need to know for the day, then goes into the office to take care of some needed paperwork, along with some accounting reports which need attention. He also updates some information on the computer. He has Ruth and another very capable worker fill in for him over two groups, so that everything will run smoothly. This turns out to be the case, and everyone has a good day there.

Meanwhile, Sarah is coordinating all the details with Alice's brother and the mortician. They plan to do just the graveside service, as a smaller number of people will be attending it, those who knew her well, along with some others who knew her from her Church ward, including Robert. Alice's brother has to make arrangements in purchasing the grave plot, as this hasn't been done previously. He also takes care of her financial account, along with her retirement account, Social Security, insurance, and related items. Sarah helps him with some of this during the few days before the service.

The day of the service comes, and after a short viewing at the church, the graveside service begins. Sarah is very emotional during this time, as Alice has been such a close family friend for many, many years. Alice's brother is also quite emotional, seeing his younger sister pass on sooner than he had thought. Both of them speak at the service. Sarah gives a special eulogy, then gives a powerfully spiritual message, which brings everyone there to tears. She feels a great peace about Alice, knowing that she's now enjoying helping others where she presently is as a spirit person.

After the service concludes, Sarah thanks everyone for coming and wishes them well. She has a good visit with Robert and thanks him again for everything he has done. As all needed items have been addressed and completed, she goes and has a quick meal, then leaves for home. She arrives in the evening, after having told Wayne and Ethan the time she will be arriving. They have dinner ready for her, and will enjoy eating all together again.

Wayne welcomes her home; he says a prayer of grace for their food, and they begin. While eating, Wayne asks his wife how everything went.

Sarah tenderly responds, "Honey, it was just wonderful. It was a very touching service. I'm so very, very happy that Ethan and I have been able to know Alice for so many years. She was such a great, wonderful person, wasn't she, Ethan."

"She sure was, Mom. I will miss her, but it's so good to know the Lord's plan for families, that we'll see her again, and that we can be blessed with much more later on."

"So, Ethan, how did everything go at work? Did you have a good experience?"

"Oh, Mom, it all went super great! I didn't mind traveling there while I was listening to some really great music in my car. Everyone did their work well. I was able to resolve any issues the group leaders had, and I completed all the reports and sent them off on time. I updated the necessary information in the computer, along with the bookkeeping, and I have everything ready for you to begin tomorrow. Mom, it's so fun learning about and doing all this. Thanks for letting me do it."

"Well, it sounds like you have everything under control. I'm so happy you enjoyed it. I really feel that, sometime, you'll make a great manager. I'm proud of your accomplishments. I bet you both missed me while I was gone, didn't you?"

Wayne tenderly responds, "I certainly did. It's so good to have you back home with me now. We are a very special family here."

Ethan then comments, "We surely are. I love you, Dad. I'm so happy you're now with my Mom." He looks at Sarah. "I also missed you. It's great having you home. I really like being around you, along with Dad."

"Thanks, Ethan. I missed both of you, too. It's so good to be back home."

Everyone settles back in all their normal routines again. Ethan is comfortable with his work, but he feels like something is missing in his life. He knows that he isn't dating much, because many of the girls he knows aren't very interested in his personality. He feels that the Lord will help him with this at the right time, that there is the special one for him later.

Ethan is quite interested in learning to play the piano, so he finds a good instructor who's also a music teacher at a local school. The teacher lives about ten minutes past his work; therefore, it would take almost an hour to go there in his car on Saturday, and to come home after meeting with him after work during the week.

Instead of commuting that far, Ethan decides to rent a small place much closer to the teacher and to work. He finds a good place, and Wayne helps him move his belongings there. He's glad that he can have his lessons and instruction more frequently now. Ethan enjoys his new Church ward, and readily makes some friends there. He is called to be the young single adult representative for his ward, which he enjoys. He's excited to go to their activities and firesides, as well. He really enjoys singing in the ward choir, along with the stake choir when they have performances. He enjoys their rehearsals, along with their performances in his ward, which they do quite often.

Ethan is picking up playing the piano rather quickly, and is excited for his rapid accomplishment. He has his own keyboard at his place, where he practices quite often. He enjoys being able to play some of his favorite music.

After moving to his own place, he calls his sister, Alexis, to see how she's doing with her schoolwork. Sarah has previously told her about Alice's passing, which saddened her, but she feels happy for her now. Ethan tells his sister about his new place, who is excited for him and says she'll come visit him soon. She tells him that she's about to graduate, and is very excited about it. She also says that she has some great news, which she will tell everyone when they can all plan to be together. Alexis says to Ethan that she is planning a time to meet with their parents and with him, and will let everybody know when it will be.

The next day, Ethan comes down with a bad cold, and ends up staying home for over a week in order to recover. He lets his mother and sister know, who tell him that they will pray for him, and they wish him well. He is able to take care of himself during this time, even though he is experiencing a great amount of discomfort. He sincerely prays that he will recover quickly, which does happen, and he thanks the Lord for blessing him.

Chapter Nine
BLESSINGS AND MIRACLES

TWO weeks after Ethan became sick, Alexis calls her parents, Sarah and Wayne, and also Ethan, and explains that she will go to his apartment to see his place and to meet with everyone there, it being more centrally located between the family home and the university. She goes and meets with all of them on the appointed Saturday. Ethan has now recovered.

Wayne and Sarah arrive after Alexis does, and hugs are exchanged all around. Everyone enjoys seeing Ethan's new place, and the way he has it decorated. They sit down and Alexis announces the date of her graduation, which will take place in three weeks. She invites them to all be there, as she receives her Bachelor of Arts degree in her major: Culinary Arts. She's very excited about it, and everyone is thrilled about her accomplishment.

Alexis then tells them, "I've already been accepted into their graduate program, where I will work toward a Master of Arts degree in exotic foods. I'm excited to do this, and I've earned enough money at my work to pay for it. I won't be needing any loan at all."

Sarah happily responds with, "Lexi, you've surely been so blessed. I'm very proud of you."

Ethan then meekly says, "You're so smart. I don't think I could ever do all that you're doing. I'm so happy you're my sister."

Alexis humbly responds, "Thank you, Ethan. I'm just doing what I can, what I enjoy doing. But you're doing so well at Mom's work. She told me earlier that you were manager for a few days there. Ethan, I've always looked up to you; you're so capable."

"Thanks, Lexi. You're a very special person to me. I've always enjoyed your cooking. I think that being the main chef at a fancy restaurant is quite an accomplishment."

"Yes, I see what you mean. Now to something more important. Mom, Dad, Ethan, I have an important announcement to make. You know I've told you about my special boyfriend I've been dating. Well, guess what? I'm engaged to him."

Sarah just about falls out of her seat. "You are? Lexi, that's so wonderful. When did this happen?"

"Just a few weeks ago, right before Ethan called me from his new place here. I wanted to wait till I had a break from school and we could all be together before I told everyone. His name is Owen Hopkinson, and he's so special. He's the best person in the world. I just can't ever stop thinking about him. He's active and very faithful in the Church. He's a great person and he really cares about me."

Sarah then excitedly asks, "When's the big day?"

"A month from now, after I graduate. Mom, everyone, he has been studying business administration, and he will be perfect to help get my restaurant started. Remember, I'm calling it, 'Lexi's Gourmet Kitchen.' He's going to help with advertising it. He works at an advertising agency right now."

"Oh, that's so wonderful," responds Sarah. "I feel he's going to be just right for you. I wish you all the success in the world. I'll be praying for you, too."

Ethan then enthusiastically says, "Lexi, I just knew you would be successful. People will love your food. You've learned so much more at school now, and I sincerely believe you'll be among the best chefs in the world."

Responding, Alexis humbly says, "I don't think I'll be *that* good, but thanks for the compliment. I just want to help people feel happy."

Wayne then comments with, "Lexi, I know for certain you'll be successful. I've been around successful entrepreneurs before, and you have all the earmarks to be one."

"Thanks, Dad. I feel so good about my life ahead of me. I know the Lord is helping me. It will be great to get started in my new career."

"I feel so happy for you," Sarah joyfully responds. "You'll be starting a new life and your career. When will we be able to meet Owen?"

"At my graduation, for sure. Maybe before, if the timing works out. I'll let you know. You will all just love him; he's so good. By the way, where's Ruth?"

"Oh, she's away, with her sister. She's taking a much needed break." Sarah glances at Ethan, then continues. "Lexi, she recently had a very bad ordeal with breast cancer, but she's in total remission and is doing very well. She's a great worker, working at the company where I work as manager, and she's progressing very quickly."

"I'm sorry to hear that she had breast cancer, but I guess we all have our trials. I've been quite sick a couple of times here, but I know that's nothing, compared to cancer. I'm happy she's better again and doing well. I remember how great she was with all of us when we were growing up. She's always been such a special friend. I hope she'll be back for my graduation."

"Oh, I'm sure she will be. I'll let her know when your graduation is, and I know she'll be overjoyed when I tell her about your wedding coming soon."

"I can just see her now. She'll be so happy to be with all

of us at these great events coming up. By the way, I brought some food with me, which Ethan quickly put away when I came today. How would you all like to have one of my specialty lunch dishes? I have this feeling you would like to celebrate this occasion."

Sarah excitedly responds, "Lexi, we certainly would! You're so thoughtful. Is there anything we can do to help?"

"There's a decorative table covering and table decorations out in my car. If you, Dad, and Ethan, can go get those and set them up; you, Mom, can help me get started in the kitchen." Alexis excitedly takes her in as she explains that she is preparing a new Asian entrée with a couple of sides, along with a special version of soup which pairs well with her gourmet dish. She explains that they wouldn't really know that it's Asian food, because it's a great step above the traditional Asian flavor. Sarah assists her with getting out the basic kitchenware, along with the food ingredients. Ethan then comes in and helps them locate some needed items.

All three of them are very excited to experience such an exquisite lunch. It's still a half hour before noon, so the three chat while Alexis methodically takes her time with cooking all the foods properly. In order for the food to taste its best, nearly an hour is needed for its preparation. There is a wonderful, exquisite aroma coming from the kitchen, and everyone is becoming more excited.

As the meal is about ready to be served, Sarah goes into the kitchen and asks, "Lexi, can I help you serve the meal? Wow, it just smells so wonderful; I can hardly wait to taste it."

"Here, Mom, you can take these in, while I bring in the rest. Be careful, it's very hot."

Sarah brings in the soup for everyone, along with some of the appetizers. She sets the food on a beautifully decorated table, where Wayne and Ethan look very happy. Alexis brings in the other appetizers, along with a special sauce which accompanies them. They both then bring in the side dishes.

Ethan says a prayer of grace and blessing for their wonderful meal. He thanks God for Alexis' great talent in preparing such tasty meals. They begin eating, and Sarah exclaims, "Wow, Lexi, wow, this is so good! I've never in my life tasted anything *this* good. Lexi, I know you are the best. You deserve an award for this." The other two applaud her as Sarah joins in. "Lexi, I know you and your restaurant will be very popular. When people go there, they'll just can't help but love your great-tasting food. You're the best!"

"Oh, Mom, you're just saying that because you're my mother, aren't you?"

"Lexi, I'm not exaggerating. I'm not saying this because you're my daughter, even though I'm glad you are. Lexi, this is definitely award-winning food. Do you all agree?"

Wayne and Ethan look up with big smiles, as they can't stop eating. Each of them nods his head in agreement. Alexis then comments, "You're just saying this now, because you're hungry. Wait until we finish the entire meal, then tell me your honest opinions, okay?"

"Alright, Lexi, we'll do that, but I know we'll definitely enjoy it."

They finish their first courses. Sarah helps clear the table while Alexis brings in their entrées. They begin, and Ethan then comments, "Lexi, you've outdone yourself. I know you are humble and modest about your cooking, because I know that's who you are. But, in reality, I feel like I'm dining in a top-of-the-line, high-end, fancy restaurant. I'm not saying that because we're related. Lexi, you know I'm very literal, as I have been all my life, and I'm truthfully saying that this food is the best I've ever had. In fact, I would love to have seconds, if there's more. I love you so much, Lexi. You're the greatest!"

"Ethan, thank you. I'm happy you like it. That means a whole lot to me."

Everyone finishes the wonderful meal which Alexis prepared for them. They sincerely thank her for providing such a great lunch. Sarah helps her with the cleanup afterward. They are all excitedly looking forward to her graduation and wedding. They visit together for a while longer, then wish her a safe trip back, as she needs to leave. She tells Ethan to keep the decorations, since they may have more meals there. Everyone thanks her again for the wonderful lunch, and she leaves.

Sarah and Ethan talk some more about the amount of humility Alexis has, along with her super, great talent, and how a great number of people will love her food when she opens her restaurant. They are all very excited about the three major events coming up in her life.

Two weeks later, Ruth comes home, and Sarah is excited to have her back at work. She's learning so well there that Sarah now has her as a regular group leader over the new workers who are beginning their jobs as new employees. These are good workers whom Sarah has interviewed and approved. Ruth is excited to be able to include this assignment in her responsibilities. She's really excited when Sarah tells her about the great events coming up for Alexis. Sarah explains that they'll take her, and all four will go to see Alexis receive her diploma.

The week goes by, and all three take the day off from work after making the necessary arrangements. They go get Ruth and they travel up to the university. They arrive in time for the graduation ceremony, where they find it very crowded. They need to walk a ways to get to their seats, which are filling up fast. When the ceremony begins, there's not an empty seat to be found. After their customary opening, the university president, along with a few deans, give their speeches. Then comes the time for the graduates to come up. Graduates from each of the colleges receive their diplomas from their respective deans. Then it's time for the College of Fine Arts. Many of the graduates of various majors come up as indicated, as each graduate's name and major is announced. Sarah is wondering when Alexis will come up. They wait while many more come, receiving their diplomas in their majors of culinary arts. Then there's a pause. Everyone in attendance waits in complete silence. The dean then says that he has a special announcement to make.

He says, "There is one more graduate to receive her diploma. Before proceeding, I need to mention that this graduate is at the top of her class, with a perfect 4.0 in the required classes in her major of culinary arts. She has also gone beyond the requirements for her major, completing much research and doing much more study in Asian and European cuisines. She has perfected some new dishes and has brought them to light here in this country, which some of the top-of-the-line chefs from here and abroad have approved with a high distinction. They have already included these new dishes in their cuisines at their respective restaurants.

"By so doing, this graduate will first be presented with an honorary award in this field, and will receive an honorary scholarship toward the completion of her Master of Arts degree. She will also receive a grant to help open her first restaurant, courtesy of these chefs.

"With great honor, and on behalf of the College of Fine Arts, I would like to present this honorary award and scholarship to Alexis Wilkinson. Please come forward."

The audience immediately applauds. Sarah is extremely surprised, along with being somewhat shocked as well. Her mouth is open wide as Ethan and Ruth look at her, then back at Alexis as she walks up. Wayne is also very pleased.

The dean gives her the award and certificate of scholarship, shakes her hand, and then says, "Alexis, please accept these as a token for all your diligent work. You are an excellent honor student here. Alexis, I would now like to present to you your diploma of graduation in your major of culinary arts." He then hands her the diploma. "I am very honored to have had the opportunity to know you and to have you as a student here. I know you'll be very successful in your future endeavors, and you will contribute greatly to our society as a whole.

Thank you very much, Alexis." He shakes her hand again as everyone applauds.

She goes back down with the other graduates and the ceremony concludes in its customary manner. Sarah, Ethan, and Ruth are awestruck, and Wayne is also quite surprised and pleased. As they were able to find seats closer to the front, they're able to go see Alexis rather quickly, despite the large crowd there.

Alexis sees them, and Sarah runs up and gives her a big hug. Through tears of joy, she says, "Lexi, what a surprise. I'm so happy for you. You're a very, very wonderful person to me. Let's see your award." She shows everyone the beautiful award she just received.

"Oh, Lexi, it's so beautiful. I'm so proud of you." Sarah gives her another hug.

Ruth has been watching all this with great excitement. She then excitedly says, "Lexi, you're so talented. I wish I could be as talented as you are. I'm so happy to know you and to see your great accomplishments."

Alexis humbly responds, "I'm just doing what I can. I love to help people be happy in the way I know how."

Sarah then comments, "Lexi, I love your modest attitude. You're doing very well, and you'll go far. Keep up the good work. I love you so much."

Ethan gives her a hug and says, "Lexi, I'm proud of you, too. Thanks for being who you are. I really appreciate all you do."

"Thanks, Ethan. Everybody, I have an announcement. One of my best chef friends here said that he will treat me and all of you with a great meal of his own, in his restaurant, to honor my graduation. It's not very far, so if you can follow me in your car, we'll go there now and have an enjoyable time."

"That sounds good to us," responds Sarah.

They go and all five enjoy the start of a wonderful time together in the restaurant. At the beginning of their meal, Alexis tells them the time of her temple wedding, and where to meet. She then says, "Everyone, I have another announcement." She gets up, walks to the adjoining aisle, and motions to a person around the corner to come in with her. They both go back to the table and she says, "Everyone, I'd like you to meet my fiancé, Owen."

Sarah stands up, shakes his hand, and says, "I'm Sarah." She gestures to Alexis and continues, "This is our wonderful daughter." Looking back, she says, "Happy to meet you, Owen."

"Glad to meet you too," he responds.

Alexis then introduces the others there. She says, "Owen, this is my father, Wayne. Here is my brother, Ethan. And over here is our great, longtime family friend, Ruth. I've known her for as long as I can remember." Owen shakes hands with each of them.

He joins them and they all enjoy their wonderful meal together. They spend this time getting to know Owen better. Everyone sees that he's a very spiritual person, and they all feel that he's just right for Alexis. They finish their meal, feeling very comfortable with him.

The following week, everyone meets at the appointed time for the wedding. Alexis first receives her temple ordinances, with her mother as her escort. Owen and Alexis then experience a marvelous, spiritual marriage ceremony in the temple, where they are beginning the process to be a forever family. After the ceremony, they go into a beautiful garden area, where Owen is wearing a very good-looking tuxedo, and Alexis is in an indescribably beautiful wedding gown. Her hair is beautifully arranged, and she looks extremely joyful. Owen's father, along with his younger brother and sister are there. His aunt and uncle are also there.

They have arranged to have an excellent photographer come. She takes many great pictures in various groupings, some of everyone, and some of just the lovely couple. One particular picture she takes is of Alexis, with Sarah and Ruth on each side of her. Very beautiful flowers, plants, and foliage surround them. Ruth desires a copy of that photo, which is promised. She just can't get over how beautiful Alexis looks.

At that moment, Ruth remembers what was told to her some time back, about her having a beautiful family after this life, and how lovely her own children will be. Looking at Alexis, she feels that she's seeing a preview of what is to come. Ruth's face becomes very emotional, and Sarah goes over to be with her, after noticing her face. Sarah puts her arm around her, and Ruth gives her a great embrace.

Ruth emotionally says, "Sarah, I'm feeling much more how it will actually be, and how I will actually feel when I will be able to have my own forever family. It's just going to be so wonderful." Her eyes are becoming more moist.

Sarah lovingly responds, "It will be very wonderful for you. Our Savior is so loving, and He loves you and will bless you with everything He has. You'll be so happy, and you'll love helping people feel happier even more. You will really be as their loving queen, and they will praise you forever. This is just a small part of what we can experience later."

"Sarah, you're such a spiritual person. I just love your spirituality, and the way you are able to bring such hope to everyone. You really are my forever friend."

"Thank you. Well, it looks like they're finishing up. Ruth, you are welcome to help us get ready for the reception. They've arranged to have a lovely garden spot in a beautiful foothills area by a little brook. This is a different place from where Wayne and I had our reception. They've also arranged to have it catered, so we can help with setting up some lovely decorations on their backdrop and around the area. How does that sound to you."

"I would love to help you with that. I'm becoming a little hungry now. I guess we'll be having lunch soon?"

"Oh, yes. I failed to mention that we'll be having a luncheon for all the family and friends at their church stake building, which will also be catered. We'll go there first, then afterward we'll pick up the decorations and load them in my SUV, and go and begin decorating. This will be so good; as you know, this is my first wedding reception for my first child's marriage in the family."

"I agree. It will be very special for everyone."

Everybody goes to the luncheon, then Sarah, Ruth, and the family go to the specified place to obtain the decorations to load up in her vehicle. They travel to the location for the reception. It is a beautiful drive going there, on a quiet country road. While driving, Sarah notices some familiarity with the area.

They arrive and everyone gets out of the vehicle to look at this pristine, wooded area. There's a special mountain scent in the air. They see the little brook nearby. There are some clouds in the sky. All this looks extremely familiar to Sarah. Wayne notices some familiarity as well.

Sarah suddenly exclaims, "I know this! An exact painting of this scene is hanging on my living room wall at home. Trish painted this scene. Wow, it's amazing, because she was never here to view this scene at all, and hasn't ever seen any pictures of it. She must have been inspired to paint this."

Wayne then says, "Remember when I told you about when I went camping with my parents when I was little? It must have been here. It looks so familiar. Look, there're some camp-sites over there. And this is where Lexi's reception will be. This is truly amazing."

Ruth and Ethan also feel very excited about all that's taking place. They're amazed as well, as they remember Trisha's painting. Everyone stands there for a few more moments, taking in all the breathtaking beauty, before going to the rented reception area to begin decorating. The backdrop is already set up. Wayne and Ethan carry the larger decorations and set them up, while Sarah and Ruth begin attaching the many smaller ones. They complete this task in plenty of time. The caterers arrive and set up the tables and some chairs, along with all their supplies. The family members and Ruth sit down to rest before people start arriving.

The members of the sound crew for the music arrive and begin their setup. Just after they finish, Owen and Alexis arrive, all dressed in their same attire as they were for the wedding pictures. Alexis sees her family and Ruth there, and goes to chat for a minute.

She says, "Hi, everyone. Wow, everything here looks so beautiful. This is the perfect place for our reception."

Sarah responds, "Yes, Lexi, everything here is beautiful, including yourself. You look so lovely. I just can't believe you're all grown up now, and married. This is certainly a day to remember."

"It sure is. Owen's family is coming in a few minutes, along with our photographer, and we'll be having more pictures taken of everyone. Mom, isn't this such a majestic location for our reception?"

"Yes, it really is. Lexi, does anything here seem familiar to you? Think hard. I know your thoughts have been involved with many things lately, but try to remember."

"Remember what, Mom? I'm not sure what you mean."

Ethan then interjects. "Lexi, remember when we were at our home, and we saw Trish's painting on the wall? Does that remind you of anything?"

Alexis suddenly realizes what Sarah was asking her. She looks around and exclaims, "Oh wow! Oh wow! This place *is* Trish's painting! How did she know? It's amazing!"

Sarah responds, "Lexi, I feel she was inspired when she painted this. She was never here. She never saw this place, nor any pictures of it. I'm feeling that this is no coincidence. I know that the Lord's hand is involved with us much more than we realize. Knowing all this makes this place even more meaningful, very, very special to you and to all of us."

"It surely is, now. I will have to tell Owen about this, and show him Trish's painting later. He will be very surprised and happy about it. Oh, I hear Owen calling me. I'll go tell him what you just told me. We'll talk some more later."

As the evening begins, many guests come to congratulate Owen and Alexis and to wish them well. They are a beautiful couple in this decorated, pristine setting. The families of the bride and groom are very well dressed also, and are up front to greet the guests. Sarah has invited Ruth to join them, for which she feels very privileged and happy.

After many of the guests have arrived, greeted the couple, and enjoyed their food, one of the sound crew goes up front to announce that they will begin some quiet music for dancing. They've been playing some very good, relaxing background music throughout the evening.

The sound crew member goes up front with a microphone he's carrying, and announces, "We are beginning some dance music now, for those who would like to dance. First, we would like to invite our newlywed couple, Owen and Alexis Hopkinson, to take the first dance, if you please."

They both go and do a slow dance to a song which is one of Ethan's favorites. They enjoy it very much, and both are smiling the entire time. Then others go and start dancing with them, including Sarah and Wayne. Ethan feels bad that Ruth is there by herself, so he asks her to dance with him, which she graciously accepts. She's very happy that Ethan has asked her to dance, and she enjoys the entire time there with him.

Everyone there has enjoyed the catered food throughout the evening. After some time has passed, there are those who are ready to leave. Owen and Alexis kindly thank everyone who came. They thank them for their gifts, and they say their goodbyes. They're ready to leave on their honeymoon. Alexis says goodbye to Sarah, Wayne, Ethan, and Ruth, thanking them for all they have done for her. Owen says goodbye to his family, and they're off. Everyone waves as they drive away.

Sarah and Wayne have recent memories of their wedding,

and this time together with Alexis and Owen brings back good memories of their own. They tell Ethan and Ruth that they're ready to leave. They all get into the SUV. Owen's family has agreed to take down the decorations and help clean up. The four travel for a while until they arrive at Ethan's place. He thanks them for everything they've done with him that day. Then they go to Ruth's place, and she thanks them as well. Sarah gives her a hug, and they leave.

Sarah and Wayne finally arrive at their home, exhausted from all the day's events. Sarah quietly mentions, "Wayne, our daughter is actually married. It's been such a big day, and now I'm really worn out. It must be that I'm older now, because twenty years ago, when I was turning thirty, I remember having much more energy at the end of the day than I do now. Oh, Wayne, don't worry. I'm not that old yet. I still have plenty of years ahead for me. I'll be fine."

"That makes me feel better," responds Wayne. "But remember, I'm about your age, also. We will just grow old together. Does that sound okay?"

"That's okay by me. I feel like getting ready for bed now, and having some extra sleep tonight. How about you?"

"It sounds like a good plan."

They have their prayer together, thanking God for keeping them safe, and for their wonderful experiences that day. Sarah asks in their prayer that Alexis and Owen will be safe, and that they will receive the blessings they deserve. She prays that everyone will sleep well that night, including Ethan and Ruth, and that they will also be blessed in their lives. She asks that she and Wayne will be protected in their daily activities, and that the Lord's Spirit will be with them, and with all their family and Ruth each day. She finishes their prayer, and they go right to sleep.

Owen's father has all the wedding gifts at his house, so after Owen and Alexis return from their honeymoon, they excitedly open their gifts. Alexis is especially excited when she discovers that some of the gifts are commercial-grade cookware for their new restaurant.

They are both very excited to locate a building for their business. They find one in the business district of the main city, close to where Ethan and Ruth live. They've also found a new house, located in the metropolis between this building and the university. This is perfect for them, as Alexis can go there when needed to do her graduate work, and still be able to have easy access to their restaurant.

Using some of her grant money, Alexis puts down a deposit to reserve the commercial building they'll be renting. She also reserves the commercial kitchen appliances which will be needed, and which will be delivered later. She plans for the indoor utilities to be modified and added, to accommodate a commercial kitchen. She also arranges to have some construction work done inside, in order to finish the kitchen, to build a seating and dining area, and to complete the main interior decorating.

While Alexis is waiting for all the paperwork and commercial food business approvals, certificates, and business license to be completed, she begins her graduate studies at the State University in accordance with her scholarship. She will be focusing on the improvement of, and the availability of less common international dishes at prestigious restaurants here in this country. She plans to do her thesis on the pairing of unique foods, as well as new, interesting combinations of less common food ingredients, which would create some new, very exotic dishes.

Alexis begins her work toward her master's degree while still working as executive chef in the current restaurant where she's employed. She earns good money there while enjoying her work. The management wants to keep her, as she is the best asset they've ever had. They knew of her plans to open her own restaurant, so they made an agreement with her that she could continue working there part-time, to help prepare some of their most difficult dishes, and have them ready for the other chefs and employees to complete.

All this is keeping Alexis very busy, but she is enjoying everything she's doing, and is happy for each new day. Owen is also assisting with getting the paperwork and certificates completed in a timely manner; however, there is a delay in receiving the approval for their food business, which results in delaying the paperwork for renting the building. This is also delaying the process of receiving the necessary certificates at the appropriate time, along with their business license, which is issued after the necessary paperwork is completed.

This is causing a small amount of frustration with Owen, as he feels that the people involved can do their jobs better than they are. On one of these evenings, after finding out there is another delay, he's feeling more irritated, and complains to Alexis.

He says to her, "Honey, I just don't understand why people can't do their jobs better. We both want to get our restaurant business open as soon as we can, but now we have to push back our plans even more, because I found out today that there's another delay in the approval for our food business. Lexi, it just isn't fair. Why does this have to happen?"

"Sweetheart, I know how this is very frustrating to you. Just know that our Savior knows everything that happens, and that it's for our experience. It will work out. We need to trust in the Lord more, and we'll be blessed. I'm looking forward to the day when we will have a successful, thriving business. It will come, I'm sure. Honey, we've already received many great, wonderful blessings, and I know we'll receive more as we stay faithful."

"I understand what you're telling me, Lexi. I can see you have very great faith. I know you're the best person for me, and you've already helped me through some difficulties. It's just that not knowing when things will happen is very difficult for me."

"I know it is. Sweetheart, let's have a prayer together right now. I know that when we ask the Lord for help with our problems, He will help us. I have seen this happen many times in my life, and He will help and comfort us as we put our faith and trust in Him."

They kneel and have a prayer together. Alexis offers the prayer, sincerely asking Heavenly Father for the help they need, along with needed blessings and comfort. She thanks God for the many blessings He has given them. Owen feels much better afterward.

The next morning, Owen receives a call from the Department of Health, telling him that their request has been approved, and they will be receiving the necessary certification soon. Owen is very excited to hear this, and calls Alexis to let her know, who is also very enthusiastic about beginning their new business. Owen then realizes this quick answer to their prayer, and he offers a silent prayer of gratitude.

Alexis has completed all her food safety management certification, and the other paperwork is now proceeding on schedule. They've obtained the lease for their building, and the approved, necessary construction and utility modification is taking place. The equipment is brought in, and everything is proceeding well. A large, very beautiful, artistic sign bearing the words, "Lexi's Gourmet Kitchen" is attached outside the building. Other signage is also placed inside the building.

The tables, chairs, and beautiful decorations are brought in and arranged in a welcoming manner. The entire interior has fresh paint and carpet, as well. Some lovely wall pictures are placed, along with copies of a couple of Trisha's best paintings. All the paperwork is complete, along with the interior of the restaurant. They now have their business license. Owen is in charge of hiring the employees, and is involved in the administration of their business. All this is complete, and they are now ready for their grand opening.

On this exciting morning, Owen has invited his family, and

Alexis has her family there, along with Ethan and Ruth. Owen has advertised this opening through many means, and has grand opening specials, coupons, and certificates, along with door prizes. The leaders from the Chamber of Commerce are there for the ribbon-cutting ceremony. There is a large crowd gathered. Many are excited to try the food there; it being well publicized, along with word being spread about the excellent food which Alexis prepares. Many already know of her excellent cooking from being customers at the restaurant where she's been working.

The ribbon-cutting ceremony begins, and the mayor begins his speech. He expresses his thanks for Alexis and her desire to provide some very excellent cuisine in the community. He also expresses his gratitude for the large turnout and community support of this venture. He says some more words of appreciation, along with his desire that this restaurant will be very successful and will be a great attraction to people from many places.

The mayor invites Alexis and Owen to come up front to the microphone, where he applauds Alexis for her great achievement in the field of culinary arts, and announces that she is the main, executive chef, and that all the dishes served will be under her supervision and approval. He invites her to say a few words in relation to her venture. Everyone applauds her as she steps in front.

She says, "I sincerely appreciate all of you coming today. I never expected such a big turnout; you are all so wonderful. I know you're looking forward to enjoying eating here. I only like helping people feel happy by doing something I love to do. I don't especially want to be rich and famous or anything like that. I just want you to be happy. Thank you."

The large group there immediately breaks out in loud applause, which continues for a minute. The mayor then says, "Thank you, Alexis, for your sweet comments. Now, if you and your husband, Owen, and you two dignitaries from our wonderful Chamber of Commerce will join us, we will all take these large scissors and cut this great ribbon in front of us, and this exciting, new restaurant, named 'Lexi's Gourmet Kitchen' will be officially open for business!" The media there comes in closer to get a good view of the happenings.

All five take hold of the scissors and gently cut the ribbon. It falls, and there is an immediate outburst of applause. The mayor thanks everyone for coming, and says, "I understand there is food ready to be served here. There are door prizes, coupons, and specials. Everything is ready for us, and I'll be one to eat some of Lexi's gourmet food. I believe that some of the members of our Chamber of Commerce will want to join me."

They go in, along with many others, including all the family members and Ruth, and the large dining area becomes completely full. The customers experience the treat of their lives as they begin their meals. They're very amazed and happy with the exquisitely tasty food they're eating. Some of the other guests there who cannot be accommodated, decide to wait for their turn. Others decide to return after a short time, as it is still a half hour before lunchtime. When these first guests finish, they tell their friends, along with the others waiting, and the word quickly spreads even more about this top-of-the-line restaurant.

Alexis is busy in her kitchen, along with two other chefs who are working under her, and there is a third cook who is assisting with quick foods, such as dinner rolls, etc. There are two employees at the cash registers, two front attendants to greet and seat people, along with six servers to take the food to the customers and to make sure their needs are being met. There are a few other workers who are involved with bussing, the clearing and cleaning of the tables, and the permanent ware and cookware cleaning. Owen has his office there in the back, where he keeps all the administrative and accounting paperwork for the employees and the restaurant, which includes inventory and the ordering of ingredients and supplies. All the workers have their necessary permits, who are involved with the food.

The cuisine there includes many international dishes, many of which are exotic. It also includes some great American dishes, including steak meals such as prime rib, porterhouse, and filet mignon. In addition, they offer less fancy, but still great-tasting dishes for those on a stricter budget. They are open all day, and serve all three meals.

The first day turns out to be a great success, with the large dining area remaining completely filled throughout the day, until closing time. Alexis is very happy with her ability to provide such great-tasting food to many people. She's happy that they enjoy her food, as well. With her assistant chefs, she is able to comfortably keep up with all the orders, and never feels stressed at all. She really enjoys cooking all that food.

The following two weeks are very similar, where the dining area is mostly always filled with happy customers. Many of them exclaim that the food there is the best they've ever tasted. They tell their friends, who also come and enjoy the same experience.

Alexis has taken vacation leave with her employment as main chef in the other restaurant during this time. Her leave time is now ending, and the management at her employment desires that she also remain there. They tell her that they've missed her, that it wasn't the same without her, and that the other chefs there weren't able to duplicate her cooking, even by following the same recipes. They explain that business has dropped off a little during her absence, and they really want her back. They know that she now has her own restaurant. They desperately desire a solution to their dilemma. Alexis tells them that according to her part-time work arrangement, she can come in early and prepare the basic, most important parts of their main entrées for them using her unique style, then keep them refrigerated until the other chefs finish them, and then complete their cooking according to the recipes. She explains that this way, the flavor she is known for will be preserved in these dishes, and their business will be great again.

The management is in full agreement with her suggestion, and thank her for her willingness to do this for them. Alexis will then go to her own restaurant and begin preparing all the exotic entrées for lunch and dinner, as her assistant chefs are able to comfortably prepare all the breakfast dishes there, by following the recipes. These are simpler dishes which they can make very tasty themselves, from the directions Alexis has given them. This way, customers will be able to enjoy her great-tasting food in two separate restaurants in two different cities. She plans to do her studies, and work on her degree in the evenings, after she's finished the main preparation of the various dishes, when her assistant chefs are able to complete them. Alexis does much of her graduate work online, and travels to the university when needed.

Doing all this puts much on the table for Alexis, so to speak, as her plate is completely full. She doesn't mind full, busy days, however, as she is thoroughly enjoying every minute of it. Of course, there are times when she becomes a bit frustrated when some supply orders don't come in on time, or when an employee has a bigger issue which needs to be resolved. During the times when she's very busy, she has Owen come and assist with issues which develop. Alexis always works on keeping a positive attitude, and remembers to frequently smile. Her associations with her mother and Ethan while growing up, as well as her remembrance of Trisha's pure love have both greatly influenced her, and many people love her friendly nature. Her husband believes that her friendliness and positivity is also increasing their business.

Owen is now working part-time at the advertising agency, and spends much of his time working in his office at their restaurant. He is finishing his degree in business administration, which he is also doing mainly during the evenings. Owen is very pleased with the way things are going for them.

Sarah and Wayne stop in frequently at the restaurant to see Alexis. They're very excited that she's doing so well. They go there during some evenings, and on Saturdays. Quite often, they get Ruth and bring her with them. There are many occasions when Ethan goes and sees his sister there. He's also happy for her and is amazed that she can do so much in a day. They all especially enjoy the food she prepares.

The restaurant is closed on Sunday, so they can attend church. Alexis and Owen desire to follow the Lord's will and live the way they should, where they know the Lord is pleased with their efforts. They both need a day in the week where they can take a break from all their work, and relax together. On one of these Sundays, Sarah and Wayne, Ethan, and Ruth go visit them in their home. This is a special time they have planned to be together as a family to share experiences, and to have a much needed visit all together.

Upon arriving, Alexis opens the door and is very happy to see the four of them there. She invites everyone inside, offers them a seat, and invites them to enjoy some hors d'oeuvres on a tray, which she has prepared. They graciously accept, and everyone enjoys what she has provided for them.

Sarah then asks, "So, Lexi, now that you have more time to visit with us, I would like to know how you are able to do so much in a day, and not be exhausted?"

She responds, "Well, I guess being young is part of it. I know much of it has to do with the fact that I really enjoy doing what I do. When that's the case, nothing that I do is really 'work' for me. It's like having fun all the time, and I feel more energy when I'm happy. What I do is quite easy for me, so I never feel stressed."

"Well, it sounds like you have it made. I'm glad you and Owen are doing so well. I've never seen such a popular place as you have. Lexi, your food easily tops any high-end restaurant I've ever been to. You have a special talent which many people really appreciate. I'm just so happy for you, and for your success you're already realizing in life."

Ruth then comments, "Lexi, I've always loved your food. I remember when you were a young teenager, and you were so excited to make dinner when you found out I was going to join all of you for dinner. That really meant a lot to me, more than you realized then. I'm so happy for you, that you're even providing a way to bring more international foods here. Your food is so much better than anything I've ever tasted before, better than any professional chef. Lexi, you are a professional."

"Thanks, Ruth. I only try my best. I just want to help people feel happy."

Wayne then says, "I agree. You do make people feel happy. I'm very happy when I have one of your delicious meals."

Then Ethan comments, "Lexi, I know everyone has different talents. It's good to put our talents to good use, for the benefit of others. Our Savior is very pleased with you and with all of us when we do this. You know that our mom has achieved great things in her work, and is now a member of the board of directors, along with being an excellent manager of all the employees in our building where we work. I really respect her for that. I love doing the bookkeeping and accounting, and by the way, Owen, we need to collaborate more, and share procedural information with each other, which may help both of us."

Owen responds, "That would be a good thing to do. I can share with you many things I've learned while studying the subject. We can talk to each other on the phone more often about this. I know you're very excellent at math. That doesn't come quite as easily to me, so there are times when I've struggled, but I've been able to make it work out in the end."

"I'd love to help you where I can, to make it easier for you. Give me a call when you have a question, and I'll do my best to help."

Sarah then says, "Let's talk about something else. How are

you two doing in your new Church ward here? Do you have any callings yet?"

"Yes, Mom, I forgot to tell you," responds Alexis. "I am the new Young Women's president."

Sarah looks shocked. "You are! Lexi, that's just wonderful! With your love of wanting to help people feel happier, I bet you're doing very well with them."

"Yes, I am. I have two of the best counselors to work with me, and they help me tremendously. We have some of the best young women here that I have ever seen. Mom, I'm so happy to do this. And don't worry about me. I'm taking care of myself and I'm getting enough sleep. I don't feel overworked. I feel our Savior is really blessing me. You taught me well all my life, and I know what is important to do, such as praying, and especially with showing Christlike love toward others."

"That's wonderful to hear. What about you, Owen. Do you have a calling at Church?"

"Actually, I've been called as a counselor in the Elders presidency. It's going very well, and I'm happy to help those who are assigned to help others feel that they have a friend."

Ruth then comments, "I feel so happy for you two. Lexi, I'm especially excited about your new calling. I remember you told me when you were a young woman yourself, you were called to be a leader over the others in your class. Apparently, the Lord knows your capabilities."

"I guess so," responds Alexis. "Well, we've been talking for a little bit, and we can talk some more, but I need to mention right now that you're all invited for dinner. I've made something that I know you'll enjoy."

"I thought I smelled something really good when we first came in here. I was only thinking it was just this food you brought to us," says Sarah, as she takes another one to eat. "These are so good. I've never had anything quite like this before."

Ruth then gratefully says, "Thank you so much, Lexi, for

inviting us to have dinner with you. You're such a special friend to me, along with all your family. This world certainly would be much better if there were more people like all of you in it."

Sarah responds, "I agree. It certainly would be better if more people follow Christ. I'm so happy that you and Owen stay so close to our Savior. I see how staying close to the Spirit of the Lord helps you with receiving daily revelation for your lives, and how that has greatly blessed your lives. I know that Christ has great plans for you."

"I know He does," responds Alexis. "We can talk more about this later, but right now I believe you'll all enjoy this new Church video which just became available. It's so good, and it has a very spiritual message. It's about how families can become forever, eternal families. I'll start it now, if you want."

They all agree, and Alexis begins the twenty-minute video. While everyone becomes extremely involved in the video, she goes into the kitchen and prepares more of her specialty dinner. A more unique, sensational aroma begins to fill the living room.

When the video concludes, everyone is feeling the Lord's Spirit very strongly. Sarah and Ruth even have some tears on their faces. Ruth says with an emotional voice, "I am even more certain now about the Lord's plan for me after this life. It will be so wonderful; I can hardly wait. I so enjoy all your friendship with me now. I've had many great experiences with you. I really know the Lord has us together for a reason. You've all helped me in so many ways. I can never thank you enough for all you have done to help me."

Sarah embraces her and then lovingly says, "Thank you, Ruth. I really consider you as a member of the family. You're a very special person, and you have a great amount of love inside you, which you show us. I can see how you've learned so much more from our Savior during the time I've known you."

With tearful eyes, Ruth responds, "Sarah, I can feel your Christlike love for me so strongly. It's just so wonderful we have a loving Savior who wants to bring us the most joy we can ever imagine. I love all of you so very much!"

Sarah notices Wayne and Ethan nearby, smiling, and nodding in full agreement. They suddenly hear Alexis calling them from the kitchen.

She announces, "Dinner's ready. Who would like to help me bring the food to the table?"

They all go in and assist her in bringing everything to the table. They've never experienced such a unique, exquisite aroma before in their lives. They sit down and Wayne offers grace and asks a blessing on their food and for each of them. They begin their dinner, and Ruth quickly exclaims, "Lexi, you've outdone yourself, again! This is so good! How did you ever come up with this?"

"Well, Ruth, I've been doing more studies and research in my graduate work. Actually, I've researched some of the best African cuisines and added my own touch, then perfected them. This is one of the best ones that I believe I'll add to my restaurant menu. What do you think about that idea?"

"I thought I recognized some similarity in native foods I had when I was young," responds Ruth. "But this is so tasty. I know everyone will like it. I think it's a great idea."

"Okay, I'll come up with a name for it, and if you don't mind, I think I'll include your name in its name. Would you like that?"

"Oh, I would love that! You're the best! I know I'll order this when I come to your restaurant. Lexi, you're such a great person. I'm so happy to have you in my life."

Sarah then says, "Lexi, you're such a thoughtful person, including Ruth in its name as you are doing. Again, this dinner is top-of-the-line for me. I can speak for all of us when I say that it needs to be added to your menu." Everyone is nodding in agreement.

Alexis responds, "Okay, it's done. I'll come up with a unique name for it, which will include the name 'Ruth,' and it will be at our restaurant this week." She looks at Ruth, and nods while she says this.

Everyone enjoys their dinner, along with a great-tasting dessert which pairs well with the meal. They have all been chatting together at the table, enjoying each other's company, when Alexis brings up the subject which Sarah was mentioning earlier, concerning the Lord's plans for them.

She asks, "Mom, before watching that great video, remember what you were saying about Christ having great plans for us as families?"

"Yes, Lexi, I do remember. You said we can talk more about it."

"Well, everyone, I have an announcement to make. I'm expecting."

Sarah just about falls off her chair, and Wayne has to hold on to her. In a moment, she regains her composure and exclaims, "Lexi, that's so wonderful to hear!"

Both Sarah and Ruth are overwhelmed. Ruth then emotionally says to her, "It's such a beautiful thing to see families continue. I've known you since you were a toddler, and now another generation is beginning. The Lord's plan is certainly true about families progressing and growing, and going on forever. I feel so much Christlike love right now; this is so wonderful."

Ethan is also happy for her. He gets up and gives his sister a hug. He says, "This is so neat. You're going to be a mother, and I'll be an uncle. I'm happy for you."

Wayne happily says, "I'm so excited and happy for you, too."

Sarah then asks, "Lexi, how is this going to work with everything you're doing already?"

She responds, "Don't worry, Mom. It's all under control. I'll take it as it happens. You've told me how Christ will help us, and I know He will help me. He has His plan for each of us, and as we follow Him and do what He wants us to do, He most certainly will bless us."

"Yes, I know. I shouldn't have questioned you about that. You're a very righteous person, and I know the Lord will bless you."

Everyone enjoys the remainder of the evening together, visiting and rejoicing over the wonderful news. Time is growing late, and nobody wants to leave, but they need to, so that they can sleep well and be rested in the morning to begin their work responsibilities. They all have a family prayer together before they leave. Sarah offers a very spiritual prayer, giving thanks for their tremendous blessings, and for the continuation of family. She offers a blessing for each of them, that the Lord's Spirit will always be with them. They then leave while feeling very uplifted. They wish Alexis and Owen well, and wave while they say goodbye. Alexis and Owen wave back, then go inside.

Owen then says, "Well, sweetheart, we sure had a fun evening. I can't get over the look on your mom's face when you told her about our new one coming. It surely was precious."

"It certainly was," Alexis responds. "They're all so happy for us. All of us need to get together more often. Family time is very important."

"I agree. When there's a time all my family can get together, we should also have them come here and have one of your special dinners with them."

"Yes, that sounds like fun. It'll be great to have them here as soon as they can. But tell them about the new addition coming to our family before then. They should know right away, because it's important. They'll be happy for us, too."

"Okay, honey, I'll do that, now that your family knows."

He kisses her, then they finish cleaning up. They spend some more relaxing time together before having their own evening prayer and going to bed.

Things are going very well for Alexis and Owen at their restaurant. They have a great amount of customers each day, who love their food. It's a successful, thriving business for them, so much so that Owen has already left his work at the advertising agency, and spends his time at the restaurant and working on his degree.

In a few months, he is ready to graduate, and he invites all his family to the ceremony. Alexis and her family are all very busy with their work and cannot attend at that particular time, as it is a very busy time of year for them. Owen understands, and says it is fine with him. He desires that their restaurant continues going strong, and knows that doing everything at once isn't possible.

Alexis continues very well with her plan of going early to the other restaurant where she is employed, and preparing the main parts of their entrées, so that they will continue to be very tasty. As a result, they have an excellent customer base there, which greatly pleases the management. She then goes to her restaurant, where people are already lining up for their lunch specials and the extravagant food there. They're excited to have her daily specials.

Alexis' pregnancy is going very well. She takes time during certain afternoons for her routine checkups, after she has prepared enough entrées to be able to take a break for a couple of hours to do this.

Sarah, Ethan, and Ruth are also doing well in their work. Business is picking up for them, and they're kept rather busy. A few workers have left, so that they can pursue other interests. Others have replaced them, along with a few more, in order to accommodate the increase in work demand. Being on the board of directors, Sarah has successfully advertised the job openings through various media. As executive manager, she interviews the candidates and selects those whom she feels are best qualified for the work, in a non-discriminatory manner.

Sarah checks in with Alexis regularly, partly to see how her work is going and to find out what new food items she's thinking about adding, but mainly to know how her pregnancy is going. Enough time has passed now, so Alexis is pleased to tell her mother that her recent ultrasound indicates that the child she's carrying is a girl. Sarah is very excited hearing this and says she'll go visit her on Saturday. After hearing this news, she tells Ethan and Ruth, who are also excited.

A little more time has passed since Sarah has been to her restaurant, so on Saturday, just before dinnertime, Sarah, Ethan, and Ruth all go to see her. Wayne has an appointment to meet with a person about selling some of his wood art he's made, so he has to stay to meet him. When they arrive at the restaurant, they find it very busy as usual. Alexis knows they're coming, so she has a place reserved for them. The attendant in the front lets her know that they have come, through their local phone system. When they're seated, Alexis comes and meets them.

Sarah gives her a hug and quietly says, "Lexi, you're showing more now. How are you feeling? Are you doing okay?"

"I'm doing fine, Mom. My doctor says so. Please don't worry. How are you doing?"

"I'm feeling very well, thank you. Lexi, you'll find out when your new one is born that you'll worry much about her. That's what mothers do. By the way, have you chosen a name for her yet?"

"Yes, we have. Last night, we agreed that her name is Rachel. How do you like it?"

"Oh, that sounds just right. It'll be so fun when she's here with us. I just can't wait. You'll be a mother, and I'll be a grandmother. It'll be wonderful! Do you know your due date?"

"As I still have about three months to go, my doctor says it should be around October 29th. That date seems familiar for some reason."

"Lexi, it should. Remember back when you were young. That day is Trish's birthday."

"Oh wow, Mom. It *is* her birthday! Wow, Rachel could

share the same birthday as her. That'll be so wonderful. Trish was such a sweet sister to me." Alexis' face is showing some emotion while saying this, as she recalls those precious memories.

Ethan and Ruth are hearing and seeing all this. Ruth then says, "I have such fond memories of Trisha. I feel that Rachel will also be very loving, a very sweet person."

Ethan then comments, "I just love that name. It's been one of my favorites for a girl's name. I'm happy you chose that name for her."

"Thank you, Ethan," she responds. "I'll need to get back to work now. Feel free to choose any complete meal each one of you would like tonight, and it's on me. My treat for you. I'll let your server know."

"Thank you very much, Lexi." Sarah gives her a hug and Alexis leaves. Sarah continues, "Okay, you both heard her. Choose your favorite meal, and we'll enjoy this time together talking, and having some very delicious food."

Their table is reserved for two hours, so all three enjoy their best food in a very relaxed setting for nearly the entire two hours, compliments of Alexis. When they're finished, they tell their server to send their goodbyes and a thank you to Alexis, who isn't able to come out and see them, as she is very busy. They go to Ethan's place and talk for a short while, then Sarah takes Ruth home, where she invites Sarah inside and asks her to stay a little longer.

Sarah agrees, and Ruth has her sit on her couch. She sits in the armchair facing her, and her cat jumps up on her lap. Ruth gently strokes her cat as she looks concerned. Noticing this, Sarah asks her, "Ruth, what's on your mind? I can see something's bothering you."

Ruth pauses for a moment, then quietly says, "Sarah, there's something that's been troubling me. You're my best friend who can understand." She lowers her head a little.

"What's wrong, Ruth?" Sarah asks in an empathetic manner. "How can I help?"

"Sarah, I'm going through a difficult time, emotionally. We just had a good time at Lexi's restaurant, where everyone enjoyed themselves. Lexi is also very happy. She was smiling much of the time. All of you are family. Even though you consider me as part of your family, I still feel very much alone." Ruth's eyes are becoming very moist, and she has a pained look on her face. Sobbing, she says, "Sarah, Lexi is soon going to be a mother. I'm glad for her, but when I saw her showing more, it just hit me right square in the face. I know about the Lord's promises for later, but…" Ruth whimpers a bit, and continues with a crying voice. "I'm all alone and I don't have any family. I won't have any kids in this life. I wasn't able to earlier, but I so wanted to be like everyone else and have the enjoyment of a good husband and a family. You don't know how lucky you are." She puts her head down and begins crying. Her cat then jumps down.

Sarah goes over to her and puts her arms around her. She hugs her for a moment while telling her that it's okay to cry. After another moment, she sits back down and gently says, while holding her hand, "Ruth, it's okay. I'm here. It's okay to let out your emotions. I remember when you told me that you feel like you're a failure in this life. I told you that our Savior has His special plan for you. I know it's hard on you right now when you see the reality of Lexi being able to have her own children. Seeing her today has triggered a flashback of the pain you were experiencing when we had that emotional talk a while back.

"Remember, I mentioned that Christ knows and is experiencing what you're feeling right now. He loves you, and has His arms outstretched toward you to comfort you. It's difficult to be reminded that you can't have a family at this time. But remember, our Savior has a very specific reason for the type of life you're living now. He isn't going to tell you exactly what that reason is, because He knows this is allowing you to increase your faith and trust in Him. This is very important. You have felt His love for you, and you know of my love for you. I care about you very much, and I truly want to help you feel happier."

Ruth is feeling a tiny bit better, but is still very sad. She responds, "Thank you for your kind words. I can feel the Lord's Spirit with you, and I feel a little better, but I just can't bear being alone here tonight. It's just too painful."

"I can feel your depression, and your great need for emotional support right now. Ruth, since tomorrow is Sunday, how would you like to come home with me tonight, and you can stay in the guest room. You can go to church with us tomorrow, and we can visit some more. I'm no longer the Relief Society president, so I don't have any extra meetings to attend. I feel that this is what you need at this moment. Would you like to do that?"

"Oh, Sarah, yes. This is exactly what I need right now. I truly appreciate the emotional support you give me. You're a very good, spiritual friend who understands me. Thank you so much."

"Okay then, go get everything together that you need to bring, everything you need for tonight and tomorrow, and I'll help you put it all in my car. It will be great to have you as a guest tomorrow."

Ruth gives her cat some food and water, along with some more attention. She gets together what she needs, and Sarah helps load it all in her car. They both leave to make the fifty-minute trip to Sarah's house. They have more time to chat while traveling. Sarah reassures her that she will give a great amount of assistance during these challenging times. She also reassures her that she's living the plan which Christ has for her right now, that her trials will never be beyond her capability to bear, and that she will never go through any trial or challenge that is not for her good. Ruth feels much more comforted after hearing this, and thanks her again for her great spirituality.

They arrive at Sarah's house, where she informs Wayne

about Ruth being a guest for the night and the next day. He's very obliging, and warmly welcomes her. On their way there, Ruth had requested that Sarah keeps their talk confidential, to which Sarah agreed. Wayne understands, however, that his wife is helping Ruth as a friend, and appreciates her doing that. After they arrive, Sarah helps Ruth bring in her belongings to the guest room.

They chat for a bit. Then all three have a wonderful prayer together before retiring for the night. Sarah sees that Ruth appears much more comfortable now, and wishes her a good sleep. She then goes into her own bedroom with Wayne. She tells him about the great meals they all had, and how Alexis covered the cost. She explains how Alexis is showing more, and they talk about how wonderful it will be when she gives birth.

Wayne then talks about the number of wood art pieces he was able to sell to the man who met with him, including a couple of nativity scenes. He tells her that this man has other acquaintances who would like to buy his work as well. Sarah is very happy that her husband is able to sell the pieces he enjoys making, and she tells him so. They talk for a while longer until they become rather sleepy. They then tell each other goodnight, wish each other a good sleep, and they kiss each other before going to sleep.

Chapter Ten

THE BEGINNING OF A FOREVER FAMILY

RUTH enjoys her time with Sarah and Wayne during the day that Sunday. They all go to Church, where they hear some very spiritual talks that are given, concerning our roles in life, how Christ can assist us, and how we can receive comfort, direction, and guidance by staying close to the Spirit of the Lord. One of the speakers mentions that by earnestly praying to Heavenly Father about our concerns, fears, worries, and difficulties in life, He will definitely hear us, and He will reach out and help us, and we can know that we can definitely trust Him and our Savior. Ruth feels very uplifted after hearing these talks, feeling much better about her life. A special musical number is also presented between the talks about Christ's great love for us. Ruth and Sarah then enjoy the discussion in their Relief Society meeting about a talk given by a Church leader concerning the ways we can feel the Lord's Spirit more in our lives. All this information is perfect for Ruth to hear at this time.

When they all arrive home, Sarah prepares a very good meal for them. While eating, they have a great conversation about the topics which were mentioned earlier at Church. Sarah shares some more inspiring information she has there at home. They also watch a few uplifting Church videos, which are helpful. At the end of the day, Ruth feels much more rejuvenated, and thanks Sarah for the wonderful time they had together. Sarah then explains that it would be better for Ruth to stay the night, as they will be heading up in the direction toward Ruth's place in the morning, to go to work.

The next morning, Ruth feels her normal self again, and is able to do her work without any difficulty. Ethan also arrives there in the morning, and welcomes his mother and Ruth, saying he is happy to see them, and he wishes them a great day. All goes very well with each of them for the next couple of months. Sarah then feels that they should all go visit Alexis at her home the next Sunday.

They arrive in the afternoon, after making plans with her for their visit. She invites them into the living room. Alexis has to use a comfortable stool, as her frontal midsection is much larger now. She offers them water, saying it's there if they would like some. Sarah then asks, "Lexi, it looks like you're close to your due date. How are you getting along?"

"Mom, I'm doing fine. However, I will need to take some time off work, starting this week. One of my assistant chefs has become very knowledgeable about my methods of preparing the various dishes, and he can now closely duplicate my exquisite, flavorful food. For sure, some of our customers will notice a little bit of a difference, but people will still enjoy visiting our restaurant."

"That's good to know. I'm happy to hear that you are taking good care of yourself during this time. I know that after Rachel is born, you'll need some extra help to take care of her, so that you can get enough sleep for the first few weeks. I know you'll be spending more time to take care of her, so I'm wondering how you're going to do your job at the other restaurant. I know I'm being too much of a mother, and that you can figure things out for yourself, but you understand my concern."

"Thanks, Mom. I plan to have my main assistant chef take my place at the other restaurant, doing the same thing I've been doing there. They're okay with him doing that, because they understand my situation. He will then be their employee, instead of me. When I'm able to return to our restaurant, the load on my assistant chef will be eased, and our customers will again enjoy my cooking, which I love to do."

Sarah then offers her support. "Wayne and I will be happy to help you with your little one at first. I'll take some vacation leave, then Wayne can continue helping when I return to work. As you know, Ethan will be able to comfortably fill in for me as manager while I'm gone. With all of us working together, everything can easily work for us." Sarah turns and looks at Ruth, who is sitting on the other side of her. "I know Ruth is very eager to help you, too. She's expressed much interest in giving Rachel her formula. This will be very helpful. In fact, I may be able to return to work sooner, and Ethan can take his vacation leave, and come here with Ruth to also help you."

"That sounds great, Mom. I really appreciate all your willingness to help. It's still a week before my due date, but I feel ready today. I understand now what you went through to have us. It's difficult, but it's special at the same time. It will be very exciting for us." Owen then goes over to her, puts his arms around her, and gives her a big hug.

Eight days later, on October 29th, Sarah receives a phone call in the morning from Owen while she's at work. He happily relates, "Sarah, I have great news! Rachel was born just after three this morning. I'm so happy. This is just wonderful. And Lexi is doing fine."

"Oh, I'm so glad to hear that. You and Lexi are now officially parents. This is wonderful news. We can come and see you and Lexi for a little bit this evening. I'll take some leave from work starting tomorrow. I just can't wait to see baby Rachel. It'll be so fun to see my first granddaughter."

"We'll be waiting for you. I'll also be letting my family know. I will talk to you some more later, when I see you."

Sarah then goes and tells Ethan and Ruth, who are working in their respective locations. They are both very excited on hearing the news, and Ruth gives her a hug. Ruth then asks if she could go into Sarah's office with her. Sarah agrees, and they both go in and close the door.

Sarah asks her, "What's on your mind?"

"I feel so happy for Lexi now. She's a mother, and I'm so happy to be able to help. You remember that I went through that experience a while ago, about feeling very depressed that I'm not able to have any children, but I know what you recently told me about Lexi allowing me to take care of Rachel, and how this would help satisfy my need to take care of a baby in this life. Sarah, in a way, I feel like she's part of my family, in a godmother sort of way, like we are all connected. I feel so happy to be able to do this."

"That's very true, Ruth. We are all families to our Savior, and it's so wonderful that we can continue on forever with even greater joy, along with your personal family later."

"Thank you, Sarah. I'm feeling so happy, and I just can't wait to see Lexi and her little one, like it is for you."

"It will be fun. We'll go after we're finished with work here. It's great that you're feeling happy. We can go back to work now, looking forward to this evening." Sarah gives Ruth a hug before she leaves, and Ruth returns to her place at work.

That evening, the three of them go to the hospital to see Alexis, Owen, and Rachel. Wayne is planning to go with Sarah in the morning, while Ethan takes Sarah's place at work. When they arrive in the evening, Sarah goes right up to Alexis and gives her a big hug. Ruth also gives her a hug.

Sarah excitedly says, "Lexi, it's so good to see you now. I bet you feel more relieved and excited. Wow, you're a mother! How does that feel?"

"Mom, it's so different. It's wonderful that I can actually

create another person. I just love the Lord's plan that we can have families and continue on. I just love my baby Rachel so much. I can't find all the words to express how I feel right now."

"I know, Lexi. I understand more about how you feel. Has anyone told you when baby Rachel will be brought back in here?"

"They told me it will be in about half an hour. Oh, Mom, she's so precious. I never thought that I could love someone so much as I love her. Of course, I love all of you, and I love our Savior, but I never felt that special type of love for a person, until I held her in my arms for the first time. It's just so indescribable."

"It surely is. When I held each of you for the first time, I felt that, too. It's so wonderful you're progressing through life like I did."

Ruth then says, "It's good to see you so happy. I can't wait till they bring Rachel. It's so wonderful to see new life. I'm very excited, along with you."

Ethan and Owen are listening to all this, waiting until they can see Rachel, when she's brought in to them. At last, the moment arrives, and the nurse brings baby Rachel to Alexis, and she gently holds her in her arms. Sarah and Ruth are right there, and both become emotional, showing great joy when they see her.

Ruth happily says, "Wow! She's so beautiful, so beautiful. She has the cutest little face." Ruth touches her tiny cheek as she is saying this.

Sarah then joyfully says, "Lexi, you have the biggest smile right now. Again, I'm so happy for you. Rachel surely is the cutest, most beautiful baby I've seen. Is it okay if I hold her for a minute?"

"Sure, here you go." Sarah gently takes baby Rachel in her arms, while supporting her tiny head which shows some hair. At that moment, Rachel makes the cutest little yawn. Everyone smiles while enjoying it. After another minute, Ruth asks if she could hold her now. Sarah gently gives Rachel to her, and Ruth's eyes begin filling with tears. She is starting to feel what it will be like when she has her own family later. Ruth then remembers how she felt when she held baby Trisha for the first time those many years ago. She feels the Lord's Spirit even stronger now. She is holding Rachel so tenderly, while looking at her cute, little face. Her eyes are closed, but her mouth begins to move to form a slight smile for a moment.

Ruth emotionally comments to Sarah, who is standing next to her. "Rachel is so happy to be here. I think she knows me, and is happy I'm holding her right now. I know she's a very special person."

Sarah agrees, and Alexis is very pleased, witnessing all that is occurring at that moment. Ethan then says, "I'd like to hold her now, if it's okay." He takes her, while supporting her tiny head. He suddenly has a flashback to when he held Trisha for the first time, when he was six years old. He feels a closeness to Rachel, as he tenderly looks at her face. He strongly feels that she's a very spiritual person, who is here now to help many people when she's older. Ethan has the thought to not say anything about this right now, but will tell Alexis later, at the right time. He then hands her back to Alexis.

Owen is standing on the other side, watching everything taking place. He's a happy father now, and is excited to see everyone there showing much joy in seeing baby Rachel. They stay for a little while, then the nurse comes in and explains that Alexis needs to spend some time alone with her baby. They wait outside the drawn curtain; the nurse then takes the baby back to the nursery. After visiting together some more, everyone is told they need to leave now, so Sarah tells her daughter that she, along with Wayne and Ruth will come back in the morning.

Bright and early they come, just after Alexis has finished her breakfast. She says, "Mom, I feel so good this morning. I was able to sleep well, and I feel so happy. Life is good."

Sarah cheerfully responds, "That's great! I remember that feeling after I gave birth to you. I assume the nurse will be bringing Rachel to us soon?"

"Yeah, in about fifteen or twenty minutes. Mom, I have so many thoughts going through my head right now. I love to be with Rachel as much as possible, but then I'm also thinking about the restaurant, and how it's doing. I know my assistant chef is handling everything okay, but I feel like I need to be there too, like it's also my baby. It's as if I want to do everything at once, but I know I can't. Maybe, sometime soon, you can go there and check with Owen, and make sure things are as they should be. Could you?"

"I understand. I'll do that for you, so you can have peace of mind. Right now, it's important to take care of Rachel. She is your responsibility at this time."

"I know. Oh, I just love her so much. She's really the most wonderful thing that's ever happened to me. It'll be so fun to watch her grow up, too. She's just so amazing."

"You're having the good experience of being a mother. As you know, this is part of the Lord's eternal plan for you." Sarah looks at Ruth, whose face is showing some mixed feelings. Sarah puts her arm around her and lovingly says, "Ruth, your time will come. I guarantee it. You will be holding Rachel in a moment, and we will greatly need your help with her in the coming days. You are very important to all of us in many ways." She gives Ruth a big hug.

Just then, the nurse brings in Rachel, and gives her to Alexis to hold. Rachel is looking very good this morning, and appears quite content. Ruth is intensely watching all this. Alexis sees and feels Ruth's emotional need, so she hands Rachel to her for a few moments. Ruth sits down with her, while looking at her lovely, cute little face. She feels a closeness to Rachel, as she gently rocks her. Ruth is beaming now, and Rachel appears even more content than she was earlier. Sarah quietly talks with Alexis during this time about how Rachel is already helping Ruth. They both see how she is responding so well. They know that Christ is helping her through this time, through Rachel.

After several minutes, Sarah notices that Ruth appears very content while holding Rachel as she's sleeping. Ruth is starting to close her eyes a bit, so Sarah takes Rachel from her, so she can hold her for a few minutes. Ruth is looking very relaxed, with a smile on her face. Sarah mentions to Alexis that Ruth will certainly be a tremendous help to them in the days ahead.

Wayne is watching all this from his chair. He's happy that Ruth is feeling better and how she is happy to be involved here. Sarah asks him if he wants to hold Rachel for a minute, which he does. He then gives her back to Alexis. They all stay for a while longer, then Sarah tells Ruth that they should now leave. All three say goodbye to Alexis, saying they'll come again tomorrow.

When they're in Sarah's vehicle, she asks, "How would you two like to go have lunch at Lexi's Gourmet Kitchen? We can make sure everything's okay there."

Ruth and Wayne are in agreement. They travel there, and are warmly greeted by the attendant in front. This person knows Sarah, and leads them back to Owen's office when she asks to see him.

They go in, and Sarah greets Owen. She says, "Owen, we just came from seeing your wife, and she's very happy. We were able to see Rachel as well, and she's the cutest little thing."

"She surely is," responds Owen. "I love her, and Lexi enjoys her so much."

"She certainly does. Lexi wanted us to come and see how you're doing today, and see how everything's going, without her being here. I know you're handling things very well, and that the workers are all doing their jobs, but we're doing this just for her peace of mind. You know how she enjoys being here more than anything else, so we've come as a favor to her. We thought we would have lunch and watch everyone in action, so we can tell her tomorrow that everything is going along fine."

"That'll be fine, Sarah. I personally know that Lexi wants everything to go smoothly, and I know that she's just going out of her mind, not being able to be here right now. It's good you came to see me. I'm happy to see you and to know we're all family together. I hope you enjoy yourselves during your lunch."

"Thanks, Owen. We'll pay for our meals today. It will be fine. Thanks for everything. We'll see you later."

They leave the office and find a good table where they're able to enjoy a great view. All three order their favorite dishes, which they enjoy. Each of them notices that the food doesn't have quite the same taste that it would normally have when Alexis is there. It's still very tasty, however, and they all enjoy this time together in a relaxed setting.

Ruth especially enjoys being able to be around Sarah, such as when they are at work, and also at times like this, where she can enjoy being with a good family. Ruth is taking her vacation leave during this time as well, so she can be of great help to Alexis.

After lunch, they go and do some needed shopping. Wayne and Sarah then help put the items which Ruth bought into her place. Sarah tells her goodbye, saying that she'll be back in the morning to go see Alexis again. Sarah and Wayne go home and take care of things which need to be done there.

The next morning, Sarah goes to see Ruth. Wayne stays in order to go to his job for part of the day, and then to do some woodworking. Sarah gets Ruth, and they go to see Alexis. She is excited to see them come into her room, and happily greets them. "Hi, Mom. Hi, Ruth. It's such a beautiful day today, isn't it? I'm told I can probably go home later today, if my doctor approves, which he probably will. Isn't that wonderful?"

"That sounds great! We can stay here and take you home

when you're approved to leave. Have you seen your Rachel yet, today?"

"Yeah, for a short time. She's so beautiful. Every time I see her, she looks even better. The nurse will be bringing her in here soon."

Ruth then comments, "Rachel is a very beautiful little girl. She seems to have a special spirit about her."

"She is very special. Well, you can hold her all you want when she's brought back. I can see you have a special connection with her."

"I really do. I know she's helping me at this time in my life."

Sarah then tenderly responds to her. "The Lord knows what is best for each of us, and He wants to help us in life. Everything happens for a reason, and I know our Savior is helping you in this way right now."

They chat for a while longer. They then hear some soft cries of a baby outside the room, and the nurse brings Rachel to them. She tells them that Rachel has been rather fussy, and she hasn't been able to calm her. Ruth asks the nurse to bring Rachel to her, which she does. Ruth slowly sits down with Rachel in her arms. She gently cradles, then slightly rocks her, and Rachel immediately stops fussing and appears more content. The nurse is very impressed with what she is seeing, and mentions that Ruth must have the magic touch. She explains that Rachel has been fed and changed, and couldn't figure out what else she needed. She then leaves the room.

Sarah and Alexis talk for a while. Sarah tells her that they went to her restaurant to have lunch yesterday. She tells her that Owen is doing fine, and all the employees are working well. She says that everything is going smoothly, but they did notice that the flavor of the food was slightly less tasty. She explains that the service was great, as always.

Alexis responds, "That's good to know, Mom. It will be great when I can be back to work, as I enjoy it so much. Some customers also want me back. Thanks for checking."

"Glad to do it. So, when you are back home, we can help you so that you can get the rest you need. Ethan is doing very well in my position at work, so I can help you for a while." She looks at Ruth, who is sitting in the chair, looking very content as she is holding Rachel. "I believe and know that Ruth will be a very great help to you and to us."

They chat for a while longer, talking about how Ruth is so good with Rachel, among other things. A bit later, the nurse comes in and explains that Alexis has been approved to be discharged to go home. They finish the paperwork, receive the necessary information, and gather all her belongings. Sarah assists Alexis, where a wheelchair is waiting. Alexis tries holding Rachel while in the wheelchair, but the ride is rather bumpy which makes Rachel fussy again, so Ruth takes her and carries her out to the parking lot. Sarah helps with carrying the belongings in a bag on her shoulder, and with pushing the wheelchair. Alexis has a car seat for the baby all ready to go, so an attendant there offers to carry the seat as they go out to Sarah's vehicle. They get all situated, then leave for the Hopkinson home.

When they arrive, Ruth brings Rachel into the house, and Sarah brings in the rest of the items while holding Alexis' hand. A crib and the nursery are already set up for Rachel, along with formula, diapers, etc. Alexis is happy to be home now. Sarah helps her get everything organized, then they relax and talk some more. Ruth is in the soft chair holding Rachel, who is very content. A short time later, Rachel is needing to be nursed, and Alexis takes her for that time. Alexis and Sarah take turns holding Rachel; however, she is much more content with Ruth for the majority of the time. Sarah really feels that the Lord is helping Ruth with her emotional needs in this way, and mentions this again to Alexis and to Ruth, who agree with Sarah.

A week passes, and Alexis is becoming more accustomed

to being a mother. Sarah and Ruth have been assisting her with the baby during the day, so that she can sleep some more. She is frequently up at night, taking care of the baby's needs. Sarah now feels that she can go back to work in her managerial position, and suggests that Ethan can take some leave now, and assist Ruth with Rachel, along with taking care of needs around the house. Alexis appreciates her brother coming to help, so that she can have the rest she needs during each day. Ethan notices that Ruth is very good with Rachel, and he feels they could be very close all their lives.

When two more weeks have gone by, Sarah tells Ethan that she needs him back at his work, and that it would be good for Ruth to return, as well. Sarah has been thinking about talking to Alexis about the plans for taking care of Rachel, and about her plans for returning to her restaurant. She arranges an evening to go talk to her about this.

On this particular evening, Sarah goes to visit Alexis and Owen in their home. Owen is in the kitchen, cleaning up. Rachel is sleeping upstairs. After greeting Alexis, they sit down in the living room. Sarah then gently asks her about their plans.

Alexis responds with, "Mom, we have been giving this much thought. One of our employees is excellent with books and accounting, and has been studying this in school. Owen has been acquainting him with our procedures; he has been assisting while Owen needed to come and help with certain items here. We now feel that this employee is capable to take his place for the present time, so that Owen can stay here with Rachel. We'll both be here at home with her for a couple of days, so that she can become more accustomed to him. Then, I'll go back to our restaurant and enjoy being a chef again."

"Lexi, that sounds like a great plan. However, there's a concern I have."

"What is it, Mom?"

"Lexi, you're a very wonderful, spiritual person. I've known this about you all your life. Now that you have your first child, it's important to be with her as much as possible. I know you love your work extremely well; however, it's very important that Rachel bonds with you during her early years. I'm not saying you have to leave your work, but this needs to be addressed, and maybe we can come up with a solution together. Does that sound like something that's agreeable to you?"

"I understand what you're saying, Mom. I now know that having children greatly changes things in life. Well, how about this? What if I work every other week? Then I can spend more time with Rachel, and still do what I enjoy."

"That sounds like a better plan. But I feel that your husband should be at your restaurant more, as it is your corporation, and you are both co-owners. I know that I shouldn't be meddling in your affairs now, but that's what mothers tend to do. You'll find that out as your family grows older. I'm just suggesting some more workable options, which I know from being in my position at work."

"Well, if I'm working there, along with Owen, who will take care of Rachel?"

"Lexi, you know that Ruth has quite a bond with her. I'll talk with her about this. I can then make arrangements with her about maybe working part-time, so that she can pay her expenses; then you and Owen can take Rachel to her before going to work. On your weeks off, Ruth will have her week to work. How does that sound?"

"I feel that will work out just fine. Oh, Mom, you're so wonderful, as always. But we don't know for sure that Ruth will want to do this."

"You saw how much she cares about Rachel while looking after her. I'm sure she'll be very excited about this plan. In fact, I'll call her right now and ask her."

Sarah calls Ruth on the phone and explains the situation to her. She is extremely excited about having the opportunity to take care of Rachel by herself during those weeks. Ruth expresses some concern about a decrease in pay. Sarah tells her that she will give her some bonus pay while she's taking care of Rachel, and that she will continue Ruth's medical insurance through a special program she's able to access. Ruth is in agreement with this, and is delighted about their plan for her with Rachel.

They end the call, and Alexis discusses with her mom what they said. Alexis then adds, "Mom, it isn't right that you should pay Ruth to take care of my little one. How about I pay half and you pay half? Is that okay with you?"

"It certainly is. Lexi, I just love your willingness to help. You've always had that in you. I really appreciate your thoughtfulness."

"Thanks, Mom. You're the best! So, next week I'll return to work, then take the following week off. I know Ruth will be overjoyed taking care of Rachel next week."

"She surely will. I'll let her know tomorrow, and we'll go ahead with our plan. It's been great working all this out with you."

Just then, Owen comes in and says, "Everything's finished in the kitchen. I feel good helping you, as I know you need your rest." He then looks over and greets Sarah.

She says, "Owen, we've come up with a good plan. Your wife can explain more of it to you later, but we've worked out a way where you can be at your restaurant much more, and make sure everything goes smoothly."

"That sounds good. Lexi can tell me all about it. I'll go check on our daughter and make sure she's okay."

"Well, it's good to see you, Owen," Sarah says while standing up. "I need to leave now. It's been wonderful talking with you, Lexi. I just know things will be fine for all of you."

"Thanks for coming. It's been fun."

Sarah gives her daughter a big hug, then waves as she says goodbye. She leaves, and Alexis goes upstairs to see her family.

Their plan is working out well for all of them. Alexis returns to work, and everybody is thrilled seeing her back, including many customers. They all congratulate her on her new daughter. She is also very excited to be there, to return to doing what she loves doing. Ruth is extremely excited to be able to care for Rachel at her own place all that week. She takes good care of her, like she's her own. Ruth feels very content and happy, and knows the Lord has answered her prayer, when she asked Him for help in feeling better about her present situation with having no family. Rachel is a very happy infant while she's with Ruth, especially when Ruth gently rocks her, sings to her, and gives her formula to her.

Sarah and Ethan are also doing very well, and are able to cover Ruth's absence on her weeks off by shifting some of the other employees' work schedules. During his free time at home, Ethan practices playing music on his keyboard, which he really enjoys. He's now able to play more of the songs he loves, along with some inspirational church hymns and some Christmas music during the season. He is continuing his lessons with his instructor, who works very well with him during some evenings and on Saturdays.

Ethan is more sociable at church, while he's there attending his meetings. He has made a few more friends, and has even befriended a family who has a son diagnosed with Asperger's Syndrome. He has given them much information to help all of them, including the notes which Sarah kept during Robert's presentation, along with the information Robert gave Sarah. Ethan told them that he is also diagnosed with this disorder, which was very interesting for them to hear. This information has helped all of them tremendously, especially their son. They have shown their great appreciation to him, and have invited him to have dinner with the family, which he enjoyed. At times, he works with their son and with all of them, when they have a question or have a need.

That Christmas season, Ethan's Church ward choir is performing several Christmas hymns and songs during the Sunday meeting in December just before Christmas. He has invited everyone to come and hear the performance. The Spencer family, the Hopkinson family, and Ruth are all there to hear Ethan and the rest of them sing their inspiring, uplifting music about Christ and His birth. Everybody is feeling very spiritually uplifted afterward, and they thank Ethan for his participation in the choir performance.

They all go to his place after the meeting to have a wonderful lunch prepared by Alexis. Everyone enjoys the great lunch and visiting during the afternoon. Ethan has his place well decorated for Christmas, with a very festive appearance. Sarah then asks him how much Christmas music he has learned to play on his keyboard.

He responds, "I've learned to play a few good ones. Would you like to hear them?"

"That would be great! I'm sure everyone will enjoy them."

Alexis then comments, "We haven't heard you play that much before now. It'll be fun to hear some good Christmas music."

Ethan starts playing a nice Christmas hymn, and everybody is surprised at how well he plays his keyboard. Rachel is very content on Ruth's lap, and all are feeling very relaxed and are smiling as they listen to his inspiring, festive music of the season. He finishes and they all applaud him. He then begins playing another one, "Angels We Have Heard on High," and Sarah suggests that everybody sing along. They stand, and Ruth gives Rachel to Owen. They begin singing, and Sarah is extremely impressed by Ruth's singing voice. She also notices Ruth's emotion as they finish singing that particular Christmas hymn.

When the song is finished, Sarah exclaims, "Ruth, I never knew you sing that well! I remember you saying that you used to sing in choirs a long time ago. You have a tremendous talent which would be good for you to share with us more often. I see you also put great feeling into your singing."

"Thank you, Sarah, for your confidence in me. I enjoy singing, but I didn't know how well I sing. This was a very touching hymn for me. Could we do another one together?"

"That's a great idea. Ethan, do you know, 'O Little Town of Bethlehem?'"

"Yes. This is one of my favorites."

They begin, and the Lord's Spirit is felt very strongly as they continue singing together. Near the end of the song, Ruth becomes very emotional as she is singing about how Christ can be so much a part of her life. Everyone notices this, and Sarah puts her arm around her. Ruth then gives her a big hug, while tears are streaming down her beautiful face. Everybody feels the Spirit so strongly, and are very moved by this touching scene.

Alexis goes up to Ruth and gently says, "Ruth, you bring such a special spirit into our families. I'm so happy you're our close friend. We all love you very much."

She tearfully responds, "Thank you, Lexi. You all bring the Spirit into my life more than I could have ever imagined." Ruth pauses for a moment while looking down as she sheds another tear. She then continues with much emotion, as her voice trembles. "I'm feeling this very strong impression I've never felt before in all my life. I strongly feel that I ... was in that great concourse of the heavenly host ... singing praises to God ... when Christ was born in Bethlehem. I now know even more that Christ really loves me, and I feel His deep love for me. Thank you all so very much."

Sarah then tenderly responds, "You are a very, very important person, Ruth. I'm seeing more of who you really are as time goes on. You're very Christlike already."

Ruth is so touched by Sarah's comment that she can't find the words to express her feelings. She sits down on the couch, and Ethan and Alexis each give her a hug, followed by Sarah. Owen has been holding Rachel, who now wants to go back to Ruth. She takes her and sheds some more tears of joy as Rachel cuddles right up to her. They all sit down and have a spiritual conversation, which includes talking about Christ's love that everyone is intensely feeling. They are all very touched by what has occurred. They enjoy chatting a while longer, sharing these tender moments together. Later in the evening, when it is time for them to leave, they tenderly thank each other for the wonderful experiences they have shared together, they hug each other, and they leave for their respective homes.

On Christmas morning, everyone meets at Wayne and Sarah's home for opening gifts and then for a good breakfast. Ruth feels so happy to be included in their festivities, and is excited for the gifts she is given. She sincerely thanks all of them. Later in the day, they all meet at the Hopkinson home for a great Christmas dinner, compliments of Alexis. Everyone shares more special moments together there, during this special day. Ruth also shares with them the precious experiences she had while celebrating Kwanzaa with her family, much earlier in her life. The others are very interested in hearing what she is telling them.

Everyone's life is going very well during the following months, except that in late winter, Alexis comes down with a very bad cold and respiratory infection, and has to be home for a couple of weeks. Owen is able to take care of any issues which come up at their restaurant during her absence. They decide that it's better for Rachel to stay with Ruth during this time, so that the baby won't become really sick, herself. Owen assists his wife while he's home, and has food and other items ready for her while he's gone, as she's extremely weak and experiencing a great amount of discomfort. Owen thinks that possibly she has worked too hard, and she isn't getting enough sleep, as she still is up during many of the nights, taking care of Rachel. He believes this has weakened her immunity, along with it being the season for more severe illnesses.

After the third week, Alexis is feeling much better. During the course of her illness, she remembers the time when she was extremely sick as a child. She remembers that she was in the hospital for a time, and had missed school for a month.

She realizes that she hasn't been getting enough sleep, and plans to take better care of herself.

Ruth has been having a wonderful experience with Rachel during this time. This little one is very accustomed to Ruth; however, Rachel seems to know her mother, and bonds to Alexis the way she should. Ruth has had some very precious moments while taking care of her. Rachel frequently looks at Ruth and smiles at her at times. She especially smiles when Ruth quietly sings to her while gently rocking her. Ruth has to get up at various times during the night to take care of her needs, so she takes naps during the day when Rachel is sleeping. This time together has been very therapeutic for Ruth.

When Alexis is well again, she goes to Ruth's place to get Rachel, who appears happy to be in her mother's arms again. Ruth tells her about the wonderful experiences they had together, which makes Alexis very happy. She tells Ruth that she will be bringing her back at the start of the week, while she goes to work again at the restaurant. She sincerely thanks Ruth for all her kindness, and wishes her well before she leaves.

When that week is over, Alexis decides to give a thank you dinner for Ruth, to show her appreciation for taking care of Rachel during the past weeks. She plans to have this at her own house, and is inviting anyone who can come. Ethan is involved with choir practice in his Church ward that particular Sunday evening, so he is unable to come. However, Sarah and Wayne go get Ruth, and they all go to see Alexis and Owen. They arrive, and they are greeted by a wonderful aroma of good food cooking. This aroma is a little different from dinners Alexis has prepared for them previously. She warmly welcomes them inside and has them go to the couches in her living room, after taking their coats.

She explains, "There's a plate of hors d'oeuvres waiting for you in there. They're my own recipe. Enjoy a few of them while I complete your dishes. You're in for a special treat tonight."

They go in and chat while enjoying the fancy, very tasty

finger food Alexis has prepared. Ruth says to Sarah and Wayne, "Wow, these are so, so good. Your daughter definitely has a tremendous talent. I believe there's no stopping her. What will she think of next?"

"Thank you, Ruth," Sarah responds. "These are even better than before. I, too, am amazed at her creativity. Everyone certainly enjoys eating her food she prepares."

"She really has a special touch, which I believe no one can duplicate, not even her other chefs in her restaurant. I'm so grateful that she invited all of us to come here for dinner tonight. I know she's doing it to show her thanks to me, for taking care of Rachel."

"Lexi really is a special person. Just like Ethan, and Trish earlier, each one of them has a special uniqueness. I can also see your own special uniqueness, Ruth. You are a very tender, loving person, and I truly appreciate everything you do for us."

Ruth's face is showing some tender emotion. "That's so kind of you to say, Sarah. You're a special person, yourself. I always feel the Spirit with you."

"I try, but I need to admit that I'm not perfect. I enjoy helping people feel better, like you do." Sarah picks up another type of food on the tray and tries it.

Ruth responds, "And I certainly enjoy being around all of you. I'm so glad we're close friends, like we are."

Sarah excitedly comments, "Wow! This one tastes even better than the one I just had. I'm sorry for not responding to you, but I just can't believe the gourmet food Lexi prepares. She tells me it's easy for her to make. I believe she'll be a grand master chef. Oh, back to what you were saying. Again, I'm sorry for not responding." Sarah looks apologetic. "I'm so happy you're my close friend, too. We've had many good times together."

"We certainly have. And you're right, these are very tasty."

Sarah then comments, "Wayne, honey, you've been rather quiet. Are you enjoying Lexi's food?"

"Yes, it's extremely good. I'm enjoying listening to both of you. I'm also enjoying the smell of Lexi's dinner she's making for us. I wonder what it will be."

Just then, Owen comes in with Rachel. When she sees Ruth, she immediately reaches one arm out toward her. He gives her to Ruth, who takes her in her arms, and Rachel cuddles right up to her. Owen goes into the kitchen to check on his wife.

Sarah tenderly comments, "I can surely see the Lord is blessing you, Ruth. You're sharing this wonderful opportunity with one of His choice spirits. I'm so happy for you."

Ruth tearfully responds, "I *am* happy. Christ certainly knows what I need and He is helping me feel good."

Alexis then calls out, "Could some of you come and help me carry these dishes out to the table, please?" Ruth places Rachel into her little carry seat. Rachel makes a couple of sounds and reaches her arms out. Ruth gently tucks her into the seat and smiles at her.

All three go in and each takes a couple of dishes of food out to the beautifully decorated table. There are plates of appetizers along with the main courses. She has prepared a three-course dinner for them. They sit down and Owen says a prayer and blessing on the food.

They begin eating while Alexis mentions, "This is a new take on some of the best German dishes. I think you'll enjoy it."

Sarah and Ruth simultaneously respond, "Wow, this is so good." They both look at each other and smile.

Alexis chuckles and says, "I'm happy you both like it. Wait till you try the other main part of it with its topping. Then let me know what you think."

They do, and are stunned. Alexis can see their reactions on their faces, which have already told her what they think about her food. She says, "I knew you'd like it."

A moment later, when Sarah has cleared her mouth, she excitedly responds, "Lexi, how in the world did you make something like this? You're right. It is a treat! I don't think I can ever have enough of it."

Ruth then comments, "I agree. I can keep eating this all day. Lexi, you're really a master chef."

"Well, I don't know about that," Alexis meekly responds. "I only learn and work on some new recipes for food that I think people will enjoy."

"You really have a winner here," remarks Sarah. "Wayne, what do you think about this meal?"

He has been eating away at his dinner. He looks up and says, "This is really, really good. I can eat every morsel. Lexi is a great chef."

Sarah then mentions, "I don't know about you, but I think some master chefs in certain prestigious restaurants will want to buy some of your recipes. What do you think about it?"

"That's possible. It may be something good to do. I'll discuss it with Owen, and we'll decide together. For now, let's enjoy this wonderful time together."

Owen says, "This idea is definitely something to look into. I'll need to do some research first. Lexi's cooking is definitely noteworthy among the top chefs."

"Okay, we'll enjoy this time together," Sarah says, "and this dinner is in honor of Ruth. She is our guest of honor tonight." She explains this while she's motioning toward Ruth.

Alexis responds, "Yes, and for that reason, I want to make sure that this is the best dinner yet."

Ruth is smiling during this acknowledgment of her. She responds, "I'm so grateful to be a friend with all of you. Each one of you is so special; I couldn't have asked for any better."

Sarah then comments, "I really feel the Lord's Spirit here with us tonight. I'm just so thankful for every one of you, and the spirit each of you brings here."

They finish this wonderful dinner and evening visiting together. Wayne, Sarah, and Ruth thank them for the food and their hospitality before leaving. On their way to Ruth's place, she talks about how she sees that Sarah and Wayne and all of them are living their lives in such a way that the Lord is very pleased with them, and that they are well on their way to becoming forever families.

Ruth looks at Sarah, and tenderly and emotionally says, "I certainly see how our Savior is blessing you, along with your husband, Wayne, and I know you will be a forever family with your children. I know that Christ is reserving this for me, later. I really know how important this is to us, and I know even more now that this is our Savior's plan."

Sarah responds, "This is such a wonderful thing to know. Everyone feels the need to have friends, and to be emotionally and spiritually connected with family. This is His plan for everyone, and you, Ruth, are included. You will have your family, as you just said."

They arrive at her place, and she invites them inside. Sarah sees that she needs to talk some more, so they agree, and all three go into her living room. Her cat comes running in.

They sit down, and Sarah asks, "Ruth, I see you show some concern when I mention about your family. Is there something more that is troubling you about this?"

"You know about my sister, Esther. She's a faithful member of the Church, but she's all I have. I've already told you about my parents, how my father is now gone, and my mother's not a member of the Church. From what I've learned in the Church, I won't belong to them after this life, considering their situation." Ruth is now showing more sadness on her face. She's also concerned about Wayne hearing all this.

Sarah responds, "It's okay that Wayne is in here. He's very understanding, and wants to be of help as well. Ruth, you know the blessings you receive in the temple. Christ has all these blessings for you as you are faithful, no matter what choices other people make in their lives. You won't be denied any of them."

Ruth lowers her head and begins to make some sobbing

sounds. Sarah puts her hand on top of hers and gently asks, "Ruth, what's the matter? Is something wrong?"

Ruth looks up at her with moist eyes and responds, with a cry in her voice. "Sarah, I've never been married in the temple. You know my previous husband divorced me a long time ago. I'm ashamed to tell you this after knowing each other for all these years, but I've never been through there." She puts her head down again.

"So that's the reason you politely wanted to wait in the guest room at the temple when Wayne and I were married. Ruth, it's okay, it's okay." Sarah goes and puts her arms around her. She embraces her for a moment, then gently asks, "Do you feel that you would like to go there soon? Do you feel ready?"

"I guess so. I don't know. Sarah, will you help me?"

"Of course I will. We'll go talk to your Church ward leader together. I'll let him know that this is your first time there. I'll help you all I can. Ruth, I care about you so much, and I sincerely want the best for you. This will be your first step on your journey to having a forever family."

Wayne then says, "I hadn't had my ordinances there either, until I met Sarah, and we were married together. Ruth, it's a wonderful experience, and you'll feel Christ's Spirit even more in your life."

Sarah adds, "When you're ready, we'll talk to your leader. When you're approved, and I'm sure you will be, I will be happy to be your escort. Ruth, it's such a wonderful experience. You'll be so very happy."

"Oh, Sarah, I want to do that. Please help me."

"Okay, we'll make the appointment with your leader. You'll need to look up your ward directory information; then I can call the secretary to plan the appointment for next Sunday. How does that sound?"

"Oh, Sarah," she repeats. "I'm nervous. This is so new to me. I really need your help."

"I understand. I'll be here for you all the way. It will be wonderful."

They talk some more before Sarah and Wayne need to leave. The next day, Ruth gives Sarah the needed information in order to make the appointment. She does, then informs Ruth about the appointment time for that Sunday at 1:30 pm. She also explains that she'll be there at Ruth's place a half hour before then, and will take her.

The time comes, and Sarah arrives at her place. Ruth is ready, with her beautiful hair arranged very attractively, and wearing a lovely Sunday dress. Sarah appears very attractive as well, in her Sunday dress. They both then go to her church building. They go in and have a good spiritual conversation while waiting by the leader's office door. A few minutes past the appointment time, the leader comes out of his office and greets the two of them. Sarah tells him that her friend, Ruth, is ready to go through the temple for the first time.

He kindly invites her into his office, where she asks, "Sarah, aren't you coming in, too?"

She responds, after indicating to the leader to wait a few seconds. "He needs to talk to you privately, but I'll be right here. It'll be okay. He's going to ask you questions about your faithfulness in following Christ. Then he will give you a paper to take to our stake leader. He needs to talk to you in private, as this is required. You're already doing just fine, so there'll be no problem. It will take just a few minutes."

She agrees, and goes in with him. After a few minutes, she comes out, appearing very happy and holding a piece of paper. She shakes hands with him and waves, while thanking him. Sarah says, "It looks like all went very well. I can see you're excited."

"I surely am!" she exclaims. "Sarah, I really feel the Spirit of the Lord with me. I feel this is what He wants me to do. However, I need to take this paper to the other leader to have it completed."

"Yes, I know. I'm planning to do that with you right now. I've already told him that you'll be coming and he is ready."

They're walking out to Sarah's vehicle and getting in as she continues talking. "This other person is going to ask you the same questions; he will then activate your paper, which you will show at the temple. We'll make an appointment for you to go there, and then I will accompany you through everything you will be doing."

"That sounds really good. It will all be so new to me; I don't know what to expect. I truly appreciate all you're doing to help me."

"I love doing this for you. Ruth, this is so extremely important to do. It's part of the Lord's plan, where you can begin your progress toward eternal glory."

Ruth feels very joyful hearing this. They talk some more, then arrive at the other building. They go inside to a waiting room near the stake offices. They are some of the first ones there. The leader comes out and warmly welcomes Ruth, and invites her into a nearby office room. They go in and talk for several minutes. When she comes out, she's really beaming, and appears to have a glow about her. The stake leader kindly thanks her for coming, and wishes both of them well as he shakes their hands.

They go outside and Ruth happily says, "Sarah, I feel so joyful. I've never felt quite this way about myself before, in all my life. Let's plan to go do this as soon as we can. I don't want to wait any longer than we need."

"Okay, I'll see if we can have an appointment at the temple this Saturday. You'll need some more clothing and items before going, so we'll go shopping before then."

Sarah makes the appointment and they do the shopping. The time comes on Saturday for them to be there, where they are warmly greeted. Sarah accompanies her with their host, and they proceed. Sarah waits for Ruth in a smaller room, after Ruth completes what she needs to do with her host. She joins Sarah, where they are given some more instruction. She appears extremely happy with what has already occurred, and about Sarah escorting her when she receives her ordinance there.

After her ordinance is completed, they both go into the most beautiful large room in the temple. Ruth is so thrilled with everything she has just completed, knowing much more about the Lord's promises and blessings for her as she stays faithful.

She joyfully and very quietly says, "Sarah, so this room is showing a little how it will be later, what I can look forward to after this life. I'm so happy here. I know I don't have to worry or wonder any more about not having a family now. You've told me that my father can receive all this here by proxy; and later, also my mother, when she accepts the Lord's gospel. Then I can be sealed to them forever. I can really be part of a forever family and have my own forever family, instead of being all by myself." Ruth begins shedding some tears of joy. "This is really becoming a reality for me. Our Savior is so kind and loving. I know so much more about His love and how to have that kind of love within us, just like Trisha showed me. I feel so wonderful."

"This truly is wonderful. I'm so happy to see your progression here," Sarah very quietly responds.

They both sit in this beautiful room for a while, enjoying the love and peace they feel. Ruth has more of a glow about her, as she feels her life is now more complete. Later, they leave, feeling rejuvenated. Sarah is very happy for Ruth's accomplishment. Ruth tells her that she wants to keep this first-time experience between them, as she doesn't want anyone but Wayne to know that she hasn't been to the temple earlier. She feels that it's not necessary for others to know this about her. All they need to know is that she can go there like the rest of Sarah's family. She also wants to keep this special time she had with Sarah there, as a private spiritual experience with her. This is because she feels that Sarah understands her much more than anyone else does.

Sarah then takes her to have a quick lunch together and talk some more. Ruth is feeling so much more included, and feels closer to Christ than she ever has. They go to Ruth's place, where she sincerely thanks Sarah for everything she has done to help her accomplish this great achievement in her life.

Sarah leaves, and Ruth goes inside and happily greets her kitty cat. She sits down and the cat immediately jumps onto her lap, and, while gently stroking it, Ruth sweetly explains to her cat everything she did that day.

Chapter Eleven

DOWN'S SYNDROME—WHAT A BLESSING

THE following few months are going very well for the Spencer and Hopkinson families, for Ethan Wilkinson, and for Ruth Shepherd. Wayne is continuing his part-time work at the library and makes beautiful works of art from wood, which some people purchase from him. Sarah is doing excellent work as executive manager in her phone and internet consulting business, as well as performing her great work as a member of the board of directors for the consulting corporation. She goes and attends weekly meetings with them; they are very pleased with all her work, and she is paid accordingly.

Sarah has kept up with the goings-on with Alexis, with her studies, with her work, and with her family. She is very happy to hear how well Alexis is doing, and expresses gratitude to the Lord for all the blessings He is giving her.

Alexis and Owen are extremely successful with their restaurant, "Lexi's Gourmet Kitchen." Alexis continues to take every other week off, in order to spend quality time with her daughter, Rachel. Even though she does this, many people flock to their restaurant, to be able to enjoy such delicious food. During the weeks she is off from work, she is on the phone many times with her main assistant chef, to work him through some details in the preparation of some of her very elegant dishes, so that their customers will hardly notice any difference in the food's flavor when she's not there to prepare these dishes herself.

Their daughter, Rachel, is growing up well, and is now over a year old. She's already learning to take a few steps, and many times she shows the cutest expressions on her face. Many people in their Church ward enjoy seeing her when they are attending their Church meetings on Sunday. Alexis is continuing her excellent work in her calling as Young Women's president. They all love her sweet disposition, and they love the activities she plans for them, by working with her two counselors. These young women also enjoy the instructors chosen for them, who teach them during their classes on Sunday.

Ethan is performing excellent work at the consulting business, where he continues working as a great group leader and bookkeeper. He assists his mother in some managerial work, as well. He is very sociable and friendly, and is able to function quite well, although he does have to settle some issues and disputes among the other workers at times, which negatively affects him a little; however, other group leaders also experience this. He tries being very Christlike around these workers. Ethan is doing very well in learning to play more music on his keyboard, and he really enjoys singing in the Church choir.

He has recently felt impressed to volunteer as a temple worker on Saturdays. He spoke to his ward and stake leaders, who recommended him to be a worker there, and he was then set apart as a temple worker by a member of the temple presidency. Ethan truly enjoys doing this work, and he is feeling his spirituality increase by doing this.

Ruth is also enjoying her work at the consulting company, and is working as a group leader. She continues to take every other week off, in order to take care of Rachel when Alexis is at work in the restaurant as master chef. She truly appreciates this time with Rachel, as it is helping her to feel much more confident with taking care of children, and it is giving her a sense of being able to raise a child, as she feels like she is participating in taking care of her own child. This is continuing to help her feel included with family, while she doesn't have any family of her own.

Ruth has been called to teach a group of four- and five-year-old children in her Church ward, along with another single woman there. She is really excited doing this, and she relates to the children very well. She is very kind and loving to them, as she fondly remembers the memories of the precious time she spent with Trisha, years ago.

She has been called upon various times by the Loveless family to help their two younger daughters with their needs. There are times when they have questions about their schoolwork, and Ruth is able to assist them in areas where she has some excellent knowledge and expertise, from when she attended public school. Lisa invites her over for dinner at times with them, which she especially enjoys. She always thanks them for their hospitality, and for their consideration of her.

At times, Esther, Ruth's sister talks to her on the phone. Ruth has told her about her experience going through the temple, for which Esther was elated. Ruth tells her more about her experiences going back there to do the necessary Lord's work as a proxy for those who are not with us anymore. She goes there many times with Ethan on Saturday, then comes back with him. There are times when he stays at her place for a little while, to talk and to enjoy the delicious soup she makes, as well as other tasty foods she is able to prepare. He thanks her for her excellent food. She enjoys doing this for him, and she enjoys his company. She is so happy for him, seeing what he's been able to accomplish in his life now, knowing how severely his Asperger's was affecting him when he was a child and teenager.

There are many times during these ensuing months when Sarah invites Ruth to have dinner with them, along with Ethan. She knows that Ruth needs to feel more a part of their family, as she is still living alone. For each of these times, Ethan goes to Ruth's place, greets her, and then takes her to the Spencer home. On one of these occasions, when Sarah had invited Ethan and Ruth to have dinner with them, Alexis happens to call Sarah and she tells her that she's coming there soon with a surprise, and to not start making any meals for them. Sarah has just informed her of this prearranged time for Ruth and Ethan to be there for dinner, so Alexis plans to give all of them an excellent meal.

On the phone, she says, "Mom, save what you were planning for dinner for another time. Owen and I are coming there with a surprise. Are Ethan and Ruth there yet?"

"They just arrived. So, Lexi, what's so special about your surprise? I already know that you're going to give us an excellent dinner."

"Just wait and see. I know you'll enjoy it. Just wait till we get there."

"Okay, we'll do that. You sure have a way to keep us guessing."

"Mom, please have Dad and Ethan come out and help us carry things in when we get there. It shouldn't be much longer."

A little more than half an hour passes, and they arrive. Wayne and Ethan go and help carry in some bags of food and some table decorations. Alexis and Owen bring in the remainder of the items, along with Rachel in her carry seat, who is sleeping. Alexis immediately begins her food preparation, after giving everyone a hug.

This occasion is a Sunday evening, so the conversation among them deals mainly with each of their experiences at church earlier in the day. Ruth talks about her Primary class of children, and how special she feels teaching them. Sarah is very happy for her. Ethan tells of his ward choir performance, and what a spiritual occasion that was for everyone.

A bit later, Owen suggests that someone helps him with decorating the table. Ruth especially enjoys doing this, so she helps him get everything ready. When they're finished, it looks beautiful, with a lovely centerpiece. A wonderful aroma of food cooking is filling the room, as is always the case when Alexis is making one of her specialties. She has her husband assist her with some of the work in the kitchen, so it will go faster and be easier for her.

Soon, her exquisite meal is ready, and Owen helps her bring everything to the table. She calls everyone to come, and the two husbands help seat their wives. Ethan assists Ruth in seating her. Wayne asks Ethan to say a prayer of grace and blessing on their food. They then look in awe at the beautiful array of their various courses of mouthwatering food, served on her exquisite serving ware. They're amazed again at how Alexis can prepare such a flavorful gourmet meal, this one being different from previous meals.

After beginning her dinner, Sarah exclaims, "Lexi, you've outdone yourself again! This is so delicious. It's simply wonderful!"

"Thanks, Mom. It's amazing what I can learn, as I continue to work on my master's degree. I'm researching and discovering so many food combinations and variations that haven't been presented anywhere, which many chefs love. I'm receiving offers from them, so they can include them in their restaurants, even from some master chefs. I'm so thankful how the Lord has helped me with what I enjoy doing. I owe it all to Him."

"That's so wonderful to hear, Lexi. I know the Lord is blessing you, as you continue to follow Christ, go to the temple, go to church and fulfill your calling, and do the other things He has asked us to do. I can see how Christ has certainly helped you in your progression throughout your life."

"Thanks. I only do what I feel is right to do, in the Lord's eyes. I also enjoy helping people have a happier day."

"I also enjoy you as my sister," Ethan comments. "I look up to you in many ways, seeing how much you have accomplished. You've graduated from college, you have a very successful business, and you have a wonderful family. I'm very happy for you."

"Thank you, Ethan. That really means a lot to me, coming from you."

"You're welcome. By the way, your dinner is excellent, as always. It's so fun to eat your meals. I always look forward to them."

Sarah notices the others eating away, and humorously says, "Lexi, I guess your food is so good, that people prefer it over conversation. Ruth, it looks like you're really enjoying your dinner."

"Yes, I am. Lexi surely has a great talent. Sorry for not talking much, but you're right. I just can't get enough of this deliciousness. It's so compelling that, at times, I forget what people are saying."

"It's okay, Ruth. We're happy that you're enjoying it so much. Remember, you're family when you're here with us, and it's okay to be more casual."

"Thank you so much. I couldn't have asked for better."

"By the way, Lexi," Sarah continues, "you haven't told us or shown us yet what your surprise is. I know it has nothing to do with your new creation you served us tonight. There's something more; am I right?"

"Mom, you know me too well. I guess this is as good of a time as any. Mom, everyone, I'm expecting again!"

Sarah is shocked and very surprised. "Wow, Lexi, I'm so excited for you! This *is* a surprise."

"I'm four months along already. I knew you'd be happy, seeing our family grow."

"I thought you looked a little different when you came in

tonight. I was only thinking that maybe you gained a little weight, from tasting all the food you cook. This is so wonderful to hear."

Ethan and Ruth are also looking very excited. Ruth joyfully says, "I'm very happy for you. I know so much more about forever families now, and I'm seeing how it's actually able to be. It'll be so fun getting to know your new one."

Ethan then says, "I'm going to be an uncle again. I'm also very happy for you."

Alexis cheerfully responds, "I knew you would all be very excited to hear about this. I just know that our Savior has great blessings in store for us as we continue to follow His will."

Everyone agrees, and they continue to enjoy each of their delicious meals while they joyfully converse about the wonderful news. They finish eating, and everyone thanks Alexis for the excellent dinner. They help clean up; they then enjoy relaxing together in the living room. Ruth is enjoying giving Rachel her food during this time, and everyone is very happy.

More than three months pass, and Alexis is showing much more now. Images have shown that the new one she is carrying is also a girl, and everyone is excited for her. The name Christine has been selected. As time is getting closer for her birth, Alexis needs to take a little more time off work, so she can rest and take care of herself. Her chief assistant chefs are more experienced with her food preparation through her explanations and their hands-on experience, so now they can more closely, and more easily duplicate her cooking procedures when she's not there. They've added another excellent chef as well, along with their other cook, to assist with cooking the smaller items when there are many customers during this time.

The time comes for her to go to the hospital. Owen takes her, and she is easily checked-in for her delivery. It is late at night on a rainy Saturday. Her husband is staying with her in the room, comforting her, as she is experiencing some discomfort with a few contractions. This turns out to be false as they subside, and she ends up waiting for what seems to be a very long time. Alexis is still not feeling very comfortable throughout this waiting period. The nurse helps her with some other medication to assist with her discomfort.

Waiting to deliver her new one this night is turning out to be much more difficult than it was with Rachel. She starts into labor again, but it's going very slowly. Owen and the nurse are helping her to feel better as much as possible. Early morning comes, and she still hasn't progressed very far. Owen sees her distress, and really feels for her. He holds her hand and becomes a bit emotional as he notices her tremendous discomfort. He says a silent prayer, asking that Alexis will be more comfortable and that Christine will come quickly. She goes into labor a little more, but she still isn't progressing very much. Her discomfort is increasing. The doctor is considering doing a C-section, but Owen and Alexis don't feel comfortable with that option.

With intense emotion, Owen then offers another prayer for her with earnestness and great faith. He immediately feels prompted to give her a priesthood blessing. He does, and is prompted to say that her present experience with such discomfort is necessary for her growth in many ways. He is inspired to bless her with the promise that Christine will be coming quickly now, and that this new spirit coming to join their family is a very special, valiant person, and will be a great blessing in their lives. He says some more precious thoughts, then concludes the blessing. Both feel the Spirit very strongly, and are quite emotional. Alexis is also noticing that her extreme discomfort has decreased a little.

A few minutes later, she begins going into labor rather quickly, with many contractions. The doctor is able to deliver Christine very easily, and both are very happy with this wonderful blessing. He cleans her and takes care of her, and puts her where she is kept warm, as the nurse cares for Alexis. He has already noticed something different about her face, but hasn't mentioned anything yet. He's waiting for the right time to tell them, as Owen and Alexis are embracing and saying comforting words to each other.

When the time is right, the doctor comes back in and sits down near the two of them. They ask him when they can see Christine. He tells them, "Owen, Alexis, you will be seeing your new daughter soon. She's being taken good care of right now. However, there's something I need to tell you."

Both of them look at each other, then back at the doctor, with their faces showing great concern. Alexis asks, "Doctor, what's wrong?" She is fearing the worst about Christine.

He responds, "She's okay, health wise. But she does have a less common condition. Alexis, Owen, your new daughter has Down's syndrome."

Alexis immediately puts her head down into her pillow and starts crying. Owen tries to comfort her, being very shocked himself. He gently puts his hands on her, but has nothing to say at the moment.

Watching this, the doctor then tells them, "I know this is difficult to hear about your new one. I have some information to give you later, but I see you need some time alone now."

The doctor leaves the room, and Owen continues his attempts to comfort his wife. He gently says, "Lexi, honey, we will get through this. I know it's an extreme shock. Please stop crying." He remembers what he said during the blessing he gave her earlier. He continues, "Honey, remember what the Lord told you in your priesthood blessing? He said Christine is a very special, valiant person, and will be a great blessing to us. I really believe that. Remember, our Savior has great blessings for you. I love you and care about you, Lexi." Owen is very emotional and tearful as he finishes speaking.

Alexis slowly looks up at him with a very wet face, her eyes quite red. Between sobs, she softly asks, "How will Christine bless us? She will be so much work for us. I don't think I'm ready to do this." She puts her head on her pillow, closes her eyes, and sobs some more.

Owen puts his hand on her shoulder and tenderly says, "Sweetheart, I will help all I can. I know the Lord has a plan for us, and He has given us Christine for a very important reason. He doesn't make mistakes. We need to trust Him and put our faith in Him, and He will bless us and help us."

Alexis looks at him again, and humbly says with great emotion, "Honey, somehow I feel you're right. This is just so unexpected. I never dreamed this would ever happen to us. I need you now more than ever. Please help me through this." Tears are running down her face.

"I sure will, sweetheart. And I know the Lord will help you, too. As you pray about this, sincerely pour out your heart to Heavenly Father, and He will listen to you and comfort you. I know He will."

"Thanks, honey. I'll do that right now." She offers a silent prayer for a few minutes. She then looks up, smiling, and says, "Wow. Heavenly Father sure answered me quickly. I can tell He completely feels my emotions. I strongly feel that what you told me is all true. I feel such great love for Christine. The Spirit has confirmed to me that she is a very spiritual person. I can't wait till I see her, and look at her beautiful face."

"It's so wonderful that you're feeling the Lord's Spirit now. I would love to look at her beautiful face, as well."

They chat for a few more minutes. Then the nurse brings in baby Christine, goes to Alexis, and puts Christine in her arms. They both notice the distinctive characteristic appearance around her eyes; however, Alexis suddenly feels a very special closeness to her. Owen can see Alexis' loving expression as she looks at their newborn's face. He also feels a close connection as he looks at Christine.

Alexis emotionally says, "Honey, Christine *is* a very special spirit. I know she was sent to us because Christ knows that we are the best for her."

"I agree. I know the Lord will help us, and things will work out well in raising her."

Both of them talk some more about their special responsibility in bringing up this precious girl in their family. They are feeling very honored, knowing that Christ has given them this opportunity to have such a spiritual person with them, who needs them. After a few more moments, Owen mentions that he needs to go home and get some sleep. Alexis says that she also needs to sleep. The nurse comes in to take baby Christine to the nursery, so she can sleep. Owen tells her that he will come back in the afternoon, and that he will let everyone know about this wonderful event. He gives his wife a hug and a kiss, then leaves.

As the sun is coming up in the morning, Sarah receives an exciting phone call from Owen. He joyfully says, "Good morning. I have some great news! Our second daughter, Christine, was born early this morning. We're all excited to see her. I'll be going back to the hospital this afternoon, but I know that you'll want to go see Lexi sooner, and see your new granddaughter. I'll probably see you there."

"Owen, that's so wonderful to hear!" exclaims Sarah. "I just can't wait to see her. I know she's very beautiful, like Rachel. Wayne and I will go see her this morning. Have you told anyone else yet?"

"Not yet. You're the first. But there's something else I need to explain."

"You can tell me when you see me," Sarah excitedly says. "I'll call Ethan and Ruth, because I'm sure they'll also want to come very soon. This is such a blessed event for our family. I'm so happy for both of you."

Sarah ends the call, then calls Ethan and Ruth. They are both very excited to hear the news. She tells Ethan to bring Ruth to the hospital, and that she will meet them both there. Ruth is extremely excited to know of the new addition to the family, and also can't wait to see her.

An hour later, everyone meets at the hospital. Sarah and

Wayne arrive shortly before Ethan and Ruth. Sarah inquires at the desk concerning the room where Alexis is. She receives the information and they quickly go to see Alexis and her newborn.

All four arrive at her room, and Sarah quietly knocks and goes in to see if she's sleeping. Alexis is partly awake. Sarah says, "Good morning, Lexi. You have some visitors who've come to see you, if that's okay." She approves, and Sarah motions for the others to come inside. They go in and happily greet Alexis.

Sarah then says, "Lexi, you look good, but I see you're a little sleepy, so we won't stay too long. How did everything go last night?"

"Oh, Mom, it was a little rough. It took several hours and I was very uncomfortable. Owen gave me a priesthood blessing, and I was much better after he'd finished. Christine then came quickly, and she's such a special spirit. It'll be fun when you get to see her. Has Owen told you about her yet?"

"No, he hasn't. What about her? Oh, he did mention that he has something to explain, but I said he can tell us here."

"Well, Mom, be prepared for this." Sarah and Ruth look inquisitively at her, showing concern. "Christine is a very extra special spirit. Heavenly Father gave her to us because she needs us. Mom, everyone, Christine has Down's syndrome."

Sarah's face shows shock. "She has what? Oh, Lexi, I'm sorry about this. You have so much to deal with, already. You don't need this too."

"Mom, Mom, it's okay," Alexis responds in a soothing manner. "I know for certain this is the Lord's plan for her and for us. I feel a very strong closeness to her, just like I do with Rachel, and with Trish and Ethan. There are many strong, very spiritual members in our families, and Christine is one of them. I feel she has this particular syndrome for her protection from this world, just like what Ethan has for him."

Ethan is appearing a bit emotional, and responds, "Thank

you, Lexi. I feel you're right. I understand the Lord's plan for me much more now. I know He has a similar plan for Christine, as well. I just can't wait to see her. She's my special niece who will be needing to understand what I know. I already feel that she's a very valiant person."

Listening to all this, Ruth responds, "I know what you're saying. I know you very well, and I feel that Rachel is such a special person already, now that she's close to turning two. I already feel a closeness to Christine, and I know she'll need me. I'll also help her as much as I can, along with each of you."

Sarah is very touched by the conversation she's hearing. She tenderly says, "It will be so wonderful to see this special, valiant member of your family. When can we see her?"

"It will be soon," responds Alexis. "The nurse said she will be bringing her, which should be in a few minutes."

A couple minutes later, the nurse comes in, carrying Christine. She gives her to Alexis, who is smiling and excited to see her again. Everyone looks at Christine's face, and they are touched by the Spirit, as they feel the radiance of her spirit. Sarah then emotionally exclaims, "I feel that Christine is so special. She has so much that she can teach us about Christ. Wow, what a very precious person she is!"

Ruth and Ethan respond in agreement. Wayne is also looking very happy, excited to see this precious new member of the family coming to join them. They talk for a bit longer, while Sarah is noticing that Alexis is becoming more sleepy. Sarah remembers this from her own deliveries, and mentions that everyone should leave for a while. The nurse then comes in to help Alexis with Christine.

They leave, but remain in the hospital area, as it would take much more travel time for everyone to go home, then return, which they felt was not sensible to do. They want to visit with Alexis some more later, when Owen is there. As it is close to lunchtime, they have some food in the cafeteria; then everyone goes to the lobby to converse some more. It is exciting for all of them as they continue remarking about Christine, and what a special person she is. Sarah gives them some inspirational messages about our Savior's plan, which she remembers from all her studies, along with what she has learned from her church meetings, and from personal experiences. She explains to them how our Savior does everything He does in perfect order, that there are reasons for what He does, and that He knows what is happening with everyone.

Sarah then says with some tenderness, "Christine is very blessed in her life. I know that Down's syndrome is a blessing to those who have this disorder in their lives, just like Ethan's disorder has been a blessing for him. I know that he wouldn't be nearly as far along as he is now, without his disorder. Our Savior certainly knows what is best for each person."

The rest of them feel Sarah's spirit as she tells them her feelings. Just then, Owen comes in, and is happy to see all of them. He asks them if they have seen Christine yet.

Sarah responds, "Yes, we have, and we are so very happy for her. We know what a great person she is."

He comments, saying, "I didn't know for sure how you would take it, but it appears you're all very excited for her. It's really a good thing to know the Lord's plans, isn't it?"

"It surely is," she replies. "Christ has such great plans for us, doesn't He? It's so wonderful to know that He will help us in life as well."

Everyone agrees; then they go back to see if Alexis is ready to see them. She is, and she welcomes everyone there. She calls the nurse about seeing Christine again, who quickly brings her. Alexis holds her for a moment, then gives her to Owen for a few moments. He feels very emotional, looking at his daughter's face. Sarah then holds her, and feels the same thing.

Ruth is very excited to hold her next, and carefully takes her. She feels a few tears of joy while looking at this newborn. She touches her tiny cheek, and suddenly Christine makes a tiny bit of a smile, with her eyes still closed. Very quietly and lovingly, Ruth tells her what a special person she is, while gently rocking her. Christine's eyes open a little bit, and while looking at them, Ruth senses the great spirituality of Christine even more. This is a very precious time for her, and everyone can see Ruth's tender, emotional expression. Sarah can especially see what a great mother Ruth will be in the life after, when she can have her own family. Ruth cradles Christine for several more moments, as everyone watches and shares this precious experience she is enjoying. They can feel Christ's love for everyone, no matter who they are. They all have tears of joy when Alexis takes Christine back in her arms.

Alexis lovingly says, "Ruth, you're such a special person, yourself. I can really feel your Christlike love. I can see it in you, just like I did with Trish. Christ hasn't forgotten you."

She emotionally responds, "Thank you so much, Lexi. That really means very much to me. You're such a sweet person." Ruth remembers through the years to the precious moments she spent with Trisha, during those two months before her passing. Tears fall, and she sobs, while saying, "It means so much, saying I have Christlike love like Trisha did. I'm so grateful to all of you. I love you so very much. Christ is very aware of me and really loves me. I know He put me here into your lives for a very important reason. I can see His tender mercies He has given me. There's no way I can thank you enough. Isn't it wonderful that our Savior has such tremendous plans for us?"

Sarah tenderly replies, "It surely is. You're such a special friend in our lives. I don't know how our lives would have been if we had never known you. I do know that it would have been much harder for us. Yes, Ruth, Christ certainly knows what He's doing."

Everyone feels the Spirit of the Lord very strongly in the room as they continue the conversation, each one adding a special thought. After a little more time has passed, the nurse comes in to check on Christine and Alexis. She feels something special in the room, and asks about it. Sarah tells her a little about what they were saying, which greatly impresses her. The nurse checks some information about Alexis, then leaves. A short time later, they finish their visit, as they see that Alexis needs to sleep some more. She thanks them for the wonderful, spiritual time they enjoyed together that Sabbath day. As they are leaving, the nurse comes in to take Christine back to the nursery, after allowing her to spend some time with Alexis.

On their way out, Owen mentions that he does need to go home right away, as his neighbor has been watching Rachel during this time, as well as the previous night. He thanks the four of them for everything they have done to help, and for the enlightening conversation. They thank him as well, and wish him a safe trip home.

Sarah and Wayne invite Ethan and Ruth to come to their house for dinner; then Sarah invites them to stay the night if they would like, so it would be easier for Ethan to go to work the next day, after taking Ruth home to her place. Owen can then bring Rachel to stay with her. They both agree this would be better, so they all go to the Spencer home and enjoy a great dinner and a relaxing time afterward, talking about their many blessings the Lord has given them. They have a family prayer later, which Ethan offers, where he expresses their gratitude for their many blessings, and especially for Christine.

Chapter Twelve
THE POWER OF PRAYER

RACHEL is intensely enjoying the time she spends with Ruth, before and after Alexis is home from the hospital. Owen is taking some time off work, in order to help his wife with their newborn. Ruth has been taking care of Rachel, who is quite a toddler, and is even beginning to say a couple of words here and there. She enjoys the simple games Ruth plays with her, and she loves the happy bedtime stories Ruth reads to her before tucking her into bed at night. She really enjoys Ruth's cooking also, and gobbles up the food she makes for a two-year-old, along with some very mild soup Ruth makes for her.

A few weeks after Christine's birth, Alexis and Owen bring her with them to visit Ruth and their daughter, Rachel. They have visited one time previously, as well. At this visit, Rachel goes right up to Alexis and excitedly says, "Mommy, Mommy." Alexis picks her up and cuddles her daughter. All three then go and have a seat in the living room. She asks Ruth how Rachel has been behaving, who tells her that she has been doing very well.

She says, "Rachel is a precious sweetheart. She's very loving, and you're lucky to have her as a member of your family.

I know she will be a tremendous help to Christine. I'm so honored to have this privilege to be able to help both of you during this time."

"I'm so happy things are going so well, and that Rachel is happy when she's not around me," responds Alexis. "You have been a great help to us, and Rachel has been a great help to you during this time. We came to visit for a little while and to spend some time with her. We also want to let you know that I'm going to begin working again at our restaurant this coming week, as I have really missed being there. Ruth, I'm wondering how it will be for you if I leave Christine with you, along with Rachel. Are you fine with that?"

"I believe it will be okay. I know she needs quite a bit of care. I think it will work."

"I've asked my mother to stop in after work to help out, so it won't be so much of a burden on you," Alexis continues. "I am figuring that you would want to take care of her also, along with Rachel, as I remember how close and loving you felt with her, right after she was born. With my mother to help, I think you'll enjoy it."

"Lexi, that sounds like a great plan. I really do love both your girls very much. I feel like both of you are family to me, and I surely enjoy your company. I will certainly miss your girls when you take your week off, but I know you need your time with them as well. I also know that I need to help your mother at her work again. You know I just love to help everyone however I can. I really feel so much more Christlike love toward people now."

"That sounds great, Ruth. Well, I'll let Mom know, so she can stop by here this coming week. I really, truly appreciate your help. You have been, and are, a lifesaver to us. Thank you so much for all you do."

Ruth lowers her head a little. She humbly responds, "You're very welcome. I just love all of you so much. I love being able to participate in the beginnings of a forever family."

Alexis and Owen stay and visit with Ruth for a while longer on this Saturday evening, as Rachel is in Ruth's lap, and Alexis is holding Christine in her arms. After their enjoyable visit, they take their two girls home with them to enjoy their Sunday together.

Early Monday, Alexis brings both girls back to Ruth, and then goes to work. All the workers give her a big welcome as she returns. She begins doing what she really enjoys doing, working as a master chef in her own restaurant. She has missed doing her famous cooking, her preparation of many exquisite dishes for about a month. Therefore, she is very excited to be able to resume her joyful activities. She gives a big "thank you" to her main assistant chef, who kept their business running well during her absence, and kept their reputation for superb dishes going strong.

The next few weeks go very well for everyone. Everything is running smoothly, and the plan for Ruth to take care of both girls every other week, with Sarah helping her after work, is working out great. During this time, Sarah feels extremely prompted by the Lord's Spirit to include a prayer for Randy, her former husband, in her daily personal prayers. She has occasionally prayed for him during the previous years. She doesn't quite understand now why she feels this prompting, but she prays for him each morning and evening, that he will live his life in such a manner so that he can receive the Lord's blessings in his life, and that he will be able to feel the Spirit of the Lord in his life more, to guide him. Sarah frequently feels this prompting, not fully understanding why, but feeling that he may be in trouble.

Being the very caring person who she is, she continues this prayer for him, sensing that maybe the Spirit will touch him, that he may change his life, and that the Lord may have a greater plan for him. She does this for the following few months, being obedient to the prompting she continues to receive through the Spirit of the Lord. Sarah has stayed close to

Christ all her life, as she knows how He can help her and guide her through numerous challenges and trials in her life. She has a strong testimony of prayer, and knows that by staying close to the Spirit, she will be inspired and guided to do the best things, which will be most beneficial for her and her family. Sarah always responds to the promptings she feels through the Spirit, knowing that she will be guided to what's right, and knowing she will never be led incorrectly by doing so.

Sarah has been sharing this feeling to pray for him with Wayne. He, too, is wondering why she is prompted to do this. He agrees that the Lord knows, and that something good may come from it. He begins to pray for him as well, and suggests that they pray for him in their prayers together, along with their personal prayers. They do this for another month. Then one Saturday, Sarah receives an unexpected phone call.

She answers, "Hello, who's this?"

Sarah is shocked when she hears the caller say, "Hello, Sarah. This is Randy Wilkinson. You are probably wondering why I'm calling you after all this time. I have this feeling I need to call you."

"You do? Why *are* you calling me?"

"Sarah, I need to apologize to you. What I did was wrong, and how I treated you is unforgiveable. I'm so sorry for what I did. Are you willing to accept my apology?"

"Well, yes, I accept your apology. Is there something happening now that is making you want to do this?"

"There certainly is. Sarah, is it okay if I come to your house, so we can talk? There's much I need to discuss and explain, and it will be much better if I do it in person. Are you still living at the same house as before, when I was with you?"

"Actually, I'm not. I've moved, and I'm now married. My husband and I can plan a time for you to come and talk with both of us. I'm okay with that."

"I'm very happy to hear that you're married. You deserve a good husband in your life. I feel so ashamed that I left you.

Would tomorrow afternoon, about two, be good for both of you? I'd love to meet your husband. Let me know your address, and I'll come and share some very important information with you."

Sarah responds, saying that would be fine. She gives him the address, wishes him well, and concludes the phone call. While talking with Wayne about this, she feels a small amount of apprehension concerning Randy coming to see her. Wayne tells her that things will be okay, that he will be right there with her. He also reminds his wife that the Spirit has prompted her to pray for him, and that this visit may have much to do concerning her prayers for him. She feels much better after hearing his comforting words.

Sunday, just a little after two in the afternoon, they hear someone knocking at their door. Wayne opens it, and sees a man standing on their front porch. He asks, "Are you Randy?"

"Yes, I am Randy. May I come in?"

"Sure, come on inside. Sarah and I have been waiting for you."

He shakes hands with him as they go into the living room. Wayne introduces himself to Randy. Sarah then comes out of the kitchen. She looks at him, and notices a rather contrite expression on his face, which now shows his age. She goes up to him and shakes hands, welcoming him there. He politely greets her. She invites him to have a seat, and Sarah sits next to Wayne, where she has a good view of Randy.

Sarah politely says, "Randy, it's good to see you after all this time. What can we do for you?"

He humbly responds, "Sarah, this may seem very strange for me to say, knowing my reputation, but I have had some things happen to me, which are very out of the ordinary, almost as if it were coming from an unseen world. I need to get your thoughts concerning this, if you desire to, as I know you're a very spiritually minded person. Do you have some time, so we can chat for a while?"

"Sure, Randy, we can talk. I'd be happy to help you understand something, if I can. What happened that's not ordinary?"

"Sarah, to help you better understand what I'll be saying, it'll be good if I start at the beginning. Later, after you help me have a better understanding of things in my life, maybe you could catch me up with what's been happening with you and the kids. But, first things first. I felt this very strong desire, apparently coming from beings unseen to me, to come and see you, almost as if my life depended on it. Isn't that strange?"

"Actually, no. When someone understands more about the Spirit World, it isn't strange at all. I'm happy for you that you had that experience and the strong desire to come and talk with me."

"Okay, I appreciate your welcoming attitude. To help you understand what I'm getting at, I'll tell you what happened to me after I left you. Remember, I was demoted at my work, and I thought that everyone was against me, including you. I felt like everything was going wrong, that I was being punished, and I couldn't handle any more problems anywhere. I was in such a bad way, and it was getting worse. I left you, and took only my clothes and personal items. As I was living out of my truck, I called my older brother, Dean, and asked him to help me. My employer was about to let me go, and not being able to handle things there anymore, I left and went to live with my brother. He saw I was in more desperate need of help than he realized.

"He took me to the doctor, who has some background in psychiatry. The doctor could see I was having a breakdown, so he gave me a medication that helped me feel much better. Dean then helped me find some work I could easily do, assisting a subcontractor in framing houses. This worked out fairly well for me, and Dean was there to help when I started having problems.

"I began having regrets leaving you, but I started feeling that you wouldn't take me back, after the way I treated you and the kids. I was too embarrassed to even show my face. So, I continued where I was, doing what I was doing.

"Dean had a very good job, working as an electrical subcontractor in the new construction of many buildings and houses. He owned an excellent truck, which contained everything he needed to do his work at the various sites. Sarah, he had it made, even though he was never married. I remember you telling me that families are important, but I didn't fully understand why. I was only doing what I thought was important, like most men do, in being married. Sarah, when I first saw you, I had the overwhelming desire to get to know you more, and to be with you as much as possible. I wanted to have a happier life than what I was having, being single. I proposed, and you accepted, which made me very happy. We were married, and I thought the joy I felt on our honeymoon would last forever. I was wrong. When we had Ethan, and you were so busy taking care of him, I felt he was more important. Then he never started talking at the appropriate age. Problems started increasing from there, and I felt they were too much for me."

Sarah is intently looking at Randy, as he becomes more emotional, showing much sadness. She gently responds, "Yes, I saw how you felt during that time, and I could see you were not handling your problems like most people do."

"And I couldn't see that anything was wrong with me. I only felt that there were too many extra problems being placed on me than what other people have. I really felt like I was being punished for something, but couldn't figure out what it was, or why.

"After starting my medication, I realized that there was something happening in my brain, which was influencing my thoughts and behaviors. The doctor told me there was an imbalance going on in my brain. The medication was helping, but there was still something else lacking. I couldn't quite figure it out. I didn't know what it was, but felt something was definitely missing.

"My brother, Dean, was never a member of the Church. He helped me in many ways, but he didn't have all the information about the gospel, like you do. Before I met you, I had a friend who introduced me to the Church, and had the missionaries teach me. Feeling that what they taught me about the gospel was more complete, I joined the Church. I had more understanding of the principles, but didn't really feel them in action, or understand how they would actually apply in my life. As you remember, Sarah, I had a difficult time trying to understand about faith, and how to have it and use it. Abstract concepts were very foreign to me, as I only understood the concrete and tangible items in this world. Intangible blessings were very difficult to grasp and recognize.

"After going to church for a while, I couldn't understand the abstract concepts any better, so I stopped going, thinking this wasn't benefitting me at all. After marrying you, I remember what you told me, that going to church has other benefits besides learning the gospel. You said that you would tell me more about what I didn't understand. You did that, but I didn't really see any other benefits. Then you said that by attending church, we can learn more about Christ, and how to become more like Him and how to be more loving toward others as He is. I felt good about that, so I listened to what was said about the subject. It made me feel good to learn more about Him. Then I saw how the members treated Ethan, and how they didn't understand him and his behaviors. This was confusing to me, as I thought they were also learning about Christ, and how to become more like Him, but they were doing the opposite. Hypocritical actions brought back bad memories of my past, and I couldn't deal with any more of it, so I needed to stay away from them. Then things escalated from there, as I didn't know what was happening in my brain.

"Sarah, you had nothing to do with my leaving you, even though I said you were compounding my problems. I sincerely apologize for that. Now, to continue with my explanation for why I'm here. I was staying with my brother in his apartment, but living on a separate floor, and paying rent to him. I was earning enough money to pay for all my needs, including groceries. I'm very thankful to him for doing this for me.

"We took our vacation trips together, with some of his other friends. Those were enjoyable times I had with him. We would go recreating in the mountains, or to some lakes and do some fishing. We also went to see some popular outdoor attractions. Dean loved riding motorcycles with his friends, and would go most weekends with them. This continued for many months. I don't enjoy that type of activity very much, so I went to the library, as I love to read books about building construction, repair, and related items.

"During one of these weekends, a law officer came to the apartment with some shocking news." Randy's face begins to show great emotion, an expression that Sarah has never seen him show at any time. He even starts shedding a few tears. He continues with a very emotional, trembling voice, one which Sarah has never heard him use. "Sarah, after confirming my name, the officer told me that my brother, Dean, had died in a traffic accident, while riding his motorcycle." Randy puts his head down and sobs a little.

Sarah tenderly says, "Randy, I'm so sorry to hear that. I know how it has been very hard on you. I see that it still is. Can I help you with this now, somehow?"

Still sobbing, he says, "I don't know. Maybe you can. I was told that he went to Heaven, or some kind of a world where spirits are. I don't know that much about it, because it's nothing tangible or concrete that I can actually see. I feel like I've lost him, and I don't have any indication that he's around at all anymore. Sarah, I really miss him, and I'm still grieving. Can you help me understand more about where he really is, so I can feel better?"

"Randy, your brother, Dean, is in a place known as the Spirit World, as a living spirit person, and he still really cares about you. We generally cannot see those who are in the Spirit World through our physical senses; however, there are those who can feel their presence around us, through feelings they experience. Dean is being taught the gospel in its completeness, and he will have the opportunity to accept the ordinances and covenants performed for him by proxy, so that he can continue progressing toward Christ and receive His blessings, if he so chooses."

Randy now appears happier. "So you're saying that someone can be baptized for him in the temple, as you once explained to me about temple baptisms, then he will be a member of the Church like I am?"

"That's right, Randy. Then he can receive the other ordinances there, as I have, in order to receive all the tremendous blessings our Savior has for him, including continuation of family. As you know, you can prepare yourself to go to the Lord's house and receive your other ordinances, so that you can continue progressing toward our Savior and receive His great blessings He has for you, including being sealed to your family forever, as you choose to do this."

"What you're saying is starting to explain a little about two dreams I had, shortly after his passing. Sarah, I was so brokenhearted after learning he was gone that I tried saying a prayer. I remember how your prayers helped me to feel better during our first few years together. I asked God to help me through my sadness and grieving, so that I could feel better. I really felt that my life was shattered, and I felt very much alone, not being married anymore, and losing my brother.

"That night I went to bed in that apartment, and I went to sleep. That particular night, however, turned out to be a very unusual one. I remember waking up sometime during the night, vividly remembering a dream I just had. The dream was about me, where I was in a very beautiful, peaceful place, and I was around many friendly people. It seemed like God was there, too. The people were telling me about the choice I had made to be born into a physical body on the Earth. They said that I would then not remember this existence, but I would have the great opportunity to continue progressing toward Christ, if I remained faithful. I could receive many blessings and would be promised even greater blessings as I did this, without remembering any of this life at all, before being born on the Earth. They also told me that Satan would do all he can to turn me away from Christ and His teachings.

"Sarah, I remember you telling me to not let Satan deceive me, and to not give in to him. I really feel that I've made a bad mistake, and now all is lost. These people in my dream told me to be very careful, or you could end up in a bad way. I started feeling very stressed; then I woke up, being very startled and very depressed. I felt extremely alone, that all was lost. I tried praying again, asking for help to be comforted.

"I felt a little better and was able to go back to sleep. I remember having another dream, this one giving me more hope. I dreamed about being in a beautiful, peaceful place again, but this time I was with my own family, and I was talking with them. I was with my wonderful wife and some children who showed me great love, which made me feel very happy, but they were not you and the children we had. I felt much better after waking up from this dream, but it left me very confused about who this family was, and where we were, while we were talking together. I asked some members I know in the Church about the meaning of this, but they weren't sure, as they don't know me that well. I thought about you, Sarah, and figured you'll probably know what this dream means. I felt very embarrassed to call you, but I want to know your thoughts about this, and I felt you would not be angry with me."

Sarah is looking at Randy's face, which is showing an expression of hope. She feels that he is more ready to understand the completeness of the gospel which has been revealed. She now knows why she was so prompted to pray for him during these past months. She knows that Randy's future life could be very dependent on what she tells him now, and she feels that the Lord guided him here, so that she can help him return to Christ. Sarah feels the weight of this great responsibility, and offers a quick, silent prayer that she will be guided by the Spirit to say the right things that would be most beneficial to him.

Sarah gently responds, "Randy, there is much that our Savior has revealed about His plans for us. I'm a forgiving person, and this is also one of the principles Christ has taught us. I would love to help you understand your mission in life here. It sounds like you have been through quite an ordeal, but I know for certain that you are not lost. Our Savior has tremendous plans for you, and through His atoning sacrifice, you are able to repent of your mistakes, and you can have the same opportunity to receive everything that God has, and have an eternal family.

"Randy, I understand the dreams you had first refer to your pre-existence, and how you chose to come to Earth, to fulfill your mission here, to follow Christ and resist Satan, without remembering anything about your pre-existence. Everyone makes mistakes, and many people don't resist the temptations of the adversary. You're not alone in the choices you made; however, our loving Savior has provided a way, through repentance, so that our mistakes can be completely gone from Christ's knowledge. As we then do the best we can to follow Christ during our lives here, we will receive great blessings.

"I understand from your second dream that you were married and sealed in the temple to a wonderful wife who is just right for you, and that you have a loving family of children who love you as their father. This family will be the beginning of great blessings you will receive, as you stay faithful in this life. What you were seeing in your dream is your family in the life after this one, where you felt great love from them. I feel that you are going to meet a wonderful, faithful woman at some point, who will be just right for you, and you will be married in the temple, and have a great family later, who will be your forever family, just like Wayne and I have. You will then begin to realize some of the most tremendous blessings you have ever experienced, which will come from your family. This will make you extremely happy. These blessings will only increase from there."

Randy now looks joyful. "Sarah, I feel something very special as you are explaining this to me. I want to feel great happiness in my life. What do I do next?"

"First of all, you will need to attend your church meetings every week. Talk to your ward bishop about any major sins, if any, and about the process of complete repentance. Work on following our Savior's teachings and keeping His commandments, which will guide all of us toward Him. Strive to be more humble, knowing that Christ knows much more about you and your potential than you do. Let Him guide you and teach you. Earnestly pray about all your desires, your fears and weaknesses, and your problems which trouble you. Listen to the promptings you receive, and then act on them. You will find that the Lord will guide you to the actions you should take in your life. You will be guided by Him much more each day, and you will begin to receive many great blessings in your life, as I have."

"That sounds rather easy to do," responds Randy. "Thanks for explaining all this to me. It really makes much sense. I'll work on doing what you told me the best I can, which I want to do now. I understand from what you're telling me, is that it comes down to the person's real intent of heart. I have seen that in you all the time I have known you. Sarah, you're telling me that you're receiving great blessings? Maybe this would be a good time to catch me up on what's been happening with you and the kids. I know they're all grown up now. How is Ethan doing with his Asperger's? I remember that was a major difficulty for him. He had nothing but one problem after another."

"He is doing very well. We met with this person who is

older than I am, and has the very same disorder. Alice introduced us to him and he gave us a presentation which lasted
for two days. He showed us how he overcame many of the
characteristics of his Asperger's, and how Ethan could do the
same, by utilizing many new techniques, through the Lord's
help. Ethan did that, and he now finds it much easier to associate and converse with people. They understand him very
well. Randy, he even served a two-year, full-time mission in
Argentina for the Church. He has a very strong testimony of
the gospel, and he loves helping people to feel better about
themselves."

"Ethan has been doing all that?" Randy responds with
great surprise. "Wow, the Lord has really blessed him. I'm now
seeing much more how Christ is able to bless people. How has
he blessed you?"

"As you see, our Savior has blessed me with an eternal
companion. We married in the temple, and the children are
all sealed to us as a forever family. Randy, remember, you can
have the same blessings. After you left, I was able to secure
excellent employment in a consulting firm. Later, I was asked
to be manager for the entire group in our building, and in
addition, was more recently asked if I wanted to be a member
of the board of directors for the corporation. I felt I could do
this, and I thank the Lord for His great blessings He gives me
as I strive to follow Him. Of course, I've had my share of trials,
which I know helps me to grow and develop in the manner
which Christ desires for me."

"Sarah, I can now see some tangible results from following
Christ. I really desire this. I definitely know that He will bless
me more in my life as I follow Him and work on being closer
to Him. I feel very happy for you."

"Thank you, Randy. I can tell you're feeling the Lord's Spirit right now. Ethan and Ruth are also receiving more blessings
in their lives, as they both work in the same business with me,
and are now group leaders. Ethan is also our bookkeeper, and

has taken on some managerial duties while I was on leave at times. He is also learning to play the piano and keyboard, and is living in his own apartment."

"I feel so good about his progression. I see how the Lord helps us to live more normal lives, and I'm glad that Ethan is able to do that. As you know, I always enjoy living life when it's more normal, without so many difficulties. I'm realizing that everyone feels that also, and I'm seeing that everyone has trials, so that they can grow and develop, as you said. Now, tell me about Lexi and Trish. How has the Lord blessed them?"

"They have been blessed in very different ways. Randy, be prepared for this, as I tell you how our Savior has blessed Trish." Sarah lowers her head a little, and shows some emotion.

"I feel something very important is happening to her. What is it, Sarah?"

"Randy, our Savior has some extremely important blessings for Trish," Sarah peacefully explains, as she continues looking emotional. "She passed away from a severe brain tumor several years ago."

Randy appears very shocked. "Oh no. Not Trish. She did? She was such a special girl. I just can't believe she's gone. I felt she would be very successful in life. It must have been very hard on all of you. I just can't believe it. I just can't." He begins to sob a little.

Sarah goes over and places her hand on his shoulder. "It's okay, Randy, it's okay. It was very difficult for us, but the Lord has blessed us, and we know she is doing some important work in the Spirit World, teaching the gospel to those there. Randy, she is such a spiritual person, full of Christlike love for everyone. I know we will see her again."

"I remember how loving and thankful she was, and I saw her always smiling. I could see something was different about her, something very special. I wish I could be more like her. I want to have the kind of love she has."

"You surely can, Randy. It is very possible as you sincerely desire to have this kind of love. Christ will help you as you earnestly pray about it. If you'd like to come over here, I want to show you something very special. You might have noticed this when you first came inside. This, Randy, is a painting that Trish made when she was ten years old. Yes, she developed her great talent she had in watercolor painting."

"Trish painted this? Wow, this is simply beautiful. I noticed it on the wall, but thought it was a painting you bought. And this plaque underneath it is so beautifully written. Oh, this picture of Trish here is so precious. Is she ten here, as well?"

"Yes, she was ten when this picture was taken. Randy, I need to tell you something special about this painting and plaque. Almost three weeks before her passing, her school put on an assembly in honor of her, honoring the special person she was, while she was still able to attend school there. They presented this painting she made, and this plaque to me at that time. They renamed the art center there in her name. It's now called 'Trisha's Art Center.' They have a copy of this paint-ing and the new name plate over the entrance." Randy is very happy now, and expresses his appreciation. "And if that's not all, the school had a fundraiser for her, where they gave me a check for over eighteen thousand dollars! I still remember how emotional I was. It covered all her medical and funeral expenses. Randy, people are very thoughtful, more than we realize."

"That's amazing! They certainly are. Sarah, I feel so happy for Trish. We all miss her, but like you said, we can see her again. I sure want to be part of a forever family now. This is so wonderful."

"I'm happy you're feeling Christ's love He has for you," Sar-ah mentions as they both sit down again. "This is such a good feeling, isn't it? Well, now about Lexi. Randy, you won't be-lieve how our Savior has blessed her. Remember how she was showing quite an interest in helping me prepare our meals?

As for her accomplishments, she has a Bachelor of Arts degree in culinary arts and is working on her Master of Arts degree. She is now married to Owen Hopkinson; she was married in the temple, and has two beautiful daughters. And if that's not enough, she and Owen have their very own restaurant, named 'Lexi's Gourmet Kitchen.' Lexi has become a certified master chef, and she prepares better, tastier, more exquisite meals than I have ever eaten anywhere. I'm not just saying that because she's a member of the family. She is becoming nationally, and even internationally recognized for her top-of-the-line dishes. She was even given a complete scholarship toward her master's degree."

Randy's mouth is partly open as he listens to Sarah explaining all of this. He enthusiastically says, "Sarah, we need to go eat there! I just can't wait to taste her food."

"Okay, we will do that. I know she will be working in her restaurant next Saturday, so we can go then. Lexi takes some weeks off, in order to spend some quality time with her girls, as she knows that families are very important, and her family is very precious to her. I'll let Ethan and Ruth know, and we can all go to have dinner together there. How does that sound?"

"That sounds wonderful to me. I feel that I have some connection to all of you, even though I'm not in the family now. We can all still be very close friends."

"We certainly can. It will be fun to have you there and share in your company. I surely feel very happy that you're turning your life around and that you'll be going to church again. I know you'll feel much better about life, you'll be happier, and you will see more of the Lord's blessings in your life."

"Sarah, I really understand what you mean. Again, I sincerely apologize for what I did to you and the kids. I'll go to my bishop and repent of all that I did, and everyone will be happy, especially me." Randy's face shows great humility.

"Randy, I forgive you, and I won't remember what you did, anymore. You're beginning a new life, and I'm excited for you.

If you like, you can stay for dinner tonight with Wayne and me, and I can invite Ethan and Ruth, and see if they're available to come. Would you like to do that?"

"I accept your invitation for dinner, and I would like to meet Ethan and Ruth again. I'm not sure what they'll think of me, however."

"Don't worry about it. I'll explain the situation to them, how you have changed, and I'm sure they'll be happy to see you again. They're both very spiritually minded, and they'll be forgiving of you, as well. Ruth can tell you some more interesting experiences she had, if she wants."

Randy agrees, and Sarah calls Ethan, then Ruth on the phone. She tells them about Randy's visit that afternoon, about all that was discussed, and about Randy's sincere change of heart. They are both very interested in hearing that he came to visit, and that he is truly repentant of what he did. Ethan tells his mom that he will get Ruth, and that they will come for dinner.

While Sarah begins her preparations for dinner, Wayne shows Randy some of his woodworking projects. Randy is very impressed with his talent, and asks him to explain in a little more detail how he was able to create certain characteristics in some of his pieces. Randy is fascinated with his explanations, and asks if he could show him later how to actually make some of these items himself. Wayne tells him that he will, and then suggests that they watch a Church video together, concerning eternal families. Randy is in agreement, and they see a very inspirational video with some powerful messages about the extreme importance of families and their purpose, and how they can go on forever in great love, and continue to increase. Randy is very touched after watching this, and he sheds a few tears of joy. He is even more determined that he will now follow the Lord's will in his own life.

Soon, Ethan and Ruth arrive, and they see Randy visiting with Wayne. Upon hearing them enter, Randy gets up and greets Ethan. While shaking hands, he joyfully says, "Ethan, is that you? Wow, you're a full-grown man now. I'm so happy to see you again." He gives him a small embrace.

Ethan responds, "I'm happy to see you, too. Mom told me you're feeling much better. I'm very excited for you. This is wonderful. You remember Ruth coming to help us? She's still a very close friend of ours, and I'm happy you can meet her again."

Randy shakes hands with her and says, "You're looking very good, Ruth. I always remember what a good person you were when I knew you then. You've been so helpful with Sarah and the kids, and I know you still are of great help to them."

She responds, "Randy, I'm glad you're doing so well. It's great that we're all friends, and that we can meet and enjoy some good times together again."

"Yes, we'll have a great evening together, and we can catch up on what's been happening in our lives. It will be very enjoyable."

Sarah then comes out and greets Ethan and Ruth, and tells everyone that dinner is about ready. They help her with getting things ready and with bringing the food to the table. They sit down and Wayne asks Randy if he would be willing to say the prayer and blessing on the food. He says that would be fine, and Randy then says a beautiful prayer and blessing, coming from his heart. Everyone is very impressed with him, seeing the change in his countenance. They all enjoy a wonderful dinner together, and everyone is happy that Randy is a good friend with them again.

Before Ethan and Ruth leave, they are told about the plan for everyone to have dinner Saturday night at Lexi's restaurant. They are excited to be there, and to see Randy meet Alexis. As they leave, they thank Sarah for the wonderful dinner, and they say their goodbyes to Randy, while shaking his hand. They thank him for his company there. Randy then leaves, after obtaining the restaurant address, and after expressing his great appreciation for their hospitality and for Sarah's encouraging words to him, along with the great dinner.

The week passes quickly, and the time arrives for their dinner at Lexi's Gourmet Kitchen. Everyone has agreed to make this a surprise for Alexis. They wait for everyone to arrive; they are then taken to their table. Sarah asks the front attendant to let Alexis know that they are there to have dinner, and to come see them when she can. Randy is amazed at the size of the restaurant and the decorations. He notices the copy of Trisha's painting there.

He excitedly says, "Lexi has certainly been blessed. I just can't believe how far she has progressed with all this. And you say she is now recognized as a certified master chef?"

"That's right," responds Sarah, "and she tells me that she is never stressed while making all her creations. I know she will be so excited to meet you now, and see how well you are doing."

Everyone looks at the menus and orders each of their favorites. Saturday evening is a very busy time there; the dining area is practically completely full. Their appetizers are brought out first, which are very tasty. Randy is already excited about the great food there. Their three-course meals arrive within fifteen minutes, and all five begin eating.

Randy is stunned as he tastes the various foods he ordered. He enthusiastically says, "Wow, wow, I have never, ever had food this good in all my life! How in the world did Lexi become so good? I just can't believe it!"

Sarah replies, "This has been her passion for a long time. She loves it and has studied much to be able to achieve everything she has done. She has tried many combinations and has perfected them. Other master chefs are now buying more of her dishes to serve at their prestigious restaurants. I believe that she will soon be famous in many more places."

"I certainly agree," responds Randy. "She definitely has a tremendous talent."

They spend their time enjoying their meals in a relaxed manner. After some time has passed, the restaurant is becoming a bit less busy. Suddenly, Alexis comes to their table, complete with her apron. She immediately sees Randy there, joyfully eating with the rest of them, and looks excited as she sees him enjoying his meal.

She greets him, saying, "Hi, Randy. It's a surprise seeing you again. You look very happy, and I can tell you're doing much better. I'm glad you came with everyone tonight. It's good to see you."

He responds, "Lexi, I am happy to be here. I made things right with your mother last Sunday, and I am happier now. It's so good to see you again, all grown up and doing very well. Lexi, your mother told me that your food excels anyone else's, anywhere. I told her that I need to come and experience it myself, so here I am. Lexi, she's right. This is the best food I've ever eaten in my entire life. How do you do it?"

She modestly replies, "Well, I just work on preparing food that will make people happy, that's all. I don't want to take all the credit for this, as I have some great assistant chefs here, and my husband works to keep everything going."

"You've certainly found the winning combination," Randy says. "I can see you're very successful, as we were noticing the crowd when we came. I know you'll go far."

"Thank you. That really means a lot to me. I'm so happy you came, and that you're enjoying your visit here. It's good to see the rest of you here, as well. How is everyone tonight?"

Sarah responds, "We are all fine, thanks. How are your girls doing?"

"Oh, Mom, Rachel is starting to talk some more. She's so excited when I'm with her and she talks to me. She really gets excited when I help her say her prayer each night, then when I tuck her in bed and read a quick bedtime story to her. I remember, Ethan, when you did that for me all those years ago. It was so special; I'll always treasure those precious times we spent together."

"Thanks, Lexi. Those were special times, and we will have many more," Ethan responds as he feels a bit of tender emotion.

"Mom, Christine is also doing better. She had a bit of a cold earlier, but she's fine now, and is also very happy when she's around me and I hold her. Both girls also really enjoy Ruth when she watches them." Alexis looks at Ruth, who is smiling. "Actually, I need to get back to work now. It's been fun seeing all of you tonight, and you too, Randy."

Everyone says goodbye and gives their thanks as Alexis goes back to the kitchen. Randy is still commenting on all the accomplishments Alexis has achieved in her life. After finishing their meals, they all say their goodbyes and return to their respective homes.

The next day, after church, Sarah receives a phone call from Randy. He tells her that he went to the meetings and thoroughly enjoyed them, and that he really felt the Lord's Spirit there. He also explains that he met with his bishop, and that past wrongdoings are all now resolved. He says that his bishop is very happy he is returning to church there, and also says that the bishop gave him a compliment, explaining how he is noticing the change in him, and how he is much more humble and wanting to learn more about Christ.

Sarah responds to him very positively, saying how excited she is for him and how well he is progressing. He tells her that he will call every Sunday afternoon, to let her know of his progress. She says that will be a good thing to do, and will look forward to his calls.

A few weeks later, Sarah comes down with a very bad case of the flu. She has to stay in bed during this time, so Ethan takes her place at work. Wayne takes good care of her, bringing her each meal and plenty of liquids, and giving her the needed medications. She ends up staying in bed for nearly two weeks, as she developed some bronchitis, and had to receive a prescription to take care of it. Later, she is able to be up, but is still very weak.

Ethan and Ruth come and visit her, which helps in cheering her up. Ethan explains to her that things are going well at work, thanks to her conducting a few needed phone calls with him, and that Ruth is doing an excellent job during the weeks she's there. He sincerely praises Ruth, while they are visiting Sarah. This makes her very pleased, and helps her feel even better about herself. Sarah agrees that she does excellent work as a group leader.

After another week, Sarah is able to return to work. Her cough has diminished somewhat, and she has enough energy to make it through the day; however, she has to rest more after returning home at the end of the day. Many of her workers are happy to see her again, and they welcome her back.

The following month, Sarah receives an exciting phone call from Randy. He joyfully says, "Guess what? Sarah, I've been approved by my ward and stake leaders in the Church to go through the temple and receive my ordinances there. Isn't that exciting?"

"It certainly is!" she enthusiastically responds. "When are you going there?"

"Next Saturday, at noon. I'm wondering if everyone can be there. I would sure like to see all of them when I receive my ordinance, if they can come."

"I will invite them all. I'm sure they will be able to come, and I know they'll be very excited for you when I tell them."

Saturday comes, and everyone arrives there an hour early. Alexis planned taking time off from her work, so she could also be there with him. Owen arrives a short time later. They get themselves ready; they assemble themselves in the designated area, and all wait for Randy to come in, to go to the instruction room. He has selected Ethan to be his escort, for which he is delighted. They finish the session together, and go into the large, most beautiful room in the temple.

Randy quietly and meekly says to them, "This experience

is so wonderful. I understand much more about Christ now, about our purpose on Earth, and what is waiting for us. I know this is where families are sealed, so they can live together in love forever, and continue progressing.

"I felt so prompted to go and talk to you that day," he quietly mentions to Sarah. "I surely understand now that people can be inspired to do good things when others earnestly pray for them. Someone must have really been praying for my welfare, when I felt inspired to go see you. I know the Lord is guiding me, and has His special plan for me. I feel so worthwhile now. I don't feel lost or alone anymore."

Sarah quietly responds, "I know He has a special plan for you, and I know He wants you to have your own eternal family. All your experiences have been for your learning, and our Savior is ready to give you more blessings."

"I agree. Ethan, I want to thank you so very much for being my escort today. I know I had a hard life, but now I feel like a completely new person. I'm so excited about my future."

"That's wonderful. It brings me great joy to see the change in you, just like I saw in many people during my mission in Argentina. The Spirit of the Lord can really change people's lives for the better, where they feel that happy Spirit in their daily lives."

Wayne, Ruth, Alexis, and Owen are also noticing the glow in Randy's countenance. They are rejoicing in him during this precious time together. Ruth and Alexis are especially joyful, having known him very well before he divorced Sarah. They, along with Ethan, have prayed for him all these years. They are now seeing the fruits of their earnest prayers for him.

Alexis and Owen invite all of them to enjoy a meal at their restaurant later, which will be on the house. Everyone's very excited. They go and have a great time together while eating their favorite foods. They're excited about Randy's new life. He tells them about how the Lord has already blessed him, in that he has received a promotion at his work, and an increase in pay. He is now able to comfortably cover all his expenses where he is presently living. He also tells them how he has recently felt his brother's presence in his life. He has experienced feelings of comfort from him, along with his guiding assistance toward correct choices.

Randy tells them that he felt the presence of someone else from the Spirit World earlier in the day, when he was still at the temple. He says, "I'm not sure who it was, but I felt such a strong feeling of tremendous love from this person."

Sarah responds, "I felt Trish's presence, when we were at the temple in that special room. It was such a sweet feeling of Christlike love, and I knew for certain it was Trish. I could feel that she is so happy that you, Randy, have accomplished this in your life. It was such a special, emotional feeling, that I couldn't mention it at the time. I'm sure this is who you felt, when you sensed that feeling of pure love."

"I know for certain you're right, Sarah. Trish was such a very loving girl when I knew her, that I felt it was almost like she was hugging me there. It was a very emotional experience, so emotional that I couldn't say anything, either."

"This is so wonderful. It stands to confirm what you've been learning and feeling, that this is the correct thing to do. You are seeing our Savior's hand in your life, and how He has been helping you."

Randy is very excited, hearing Sarah's confirmation about what he has been saying. Ethan and Ruth also mention that they felt Trisha's presence, and Alexis later tells them about the special experience she had, while feeling Trisha there.

Chapter Thirteen

The Road to Your Forever Family

A few months have now gone by since Randy received his temple ordinances. He has been staying in contact with Sarah by phone every week, keeping her updated with his progress. He has been going back to the temple frequently, to do other ordinance work for some of his ancestors he has researched. A few members in his Church ward have helped him with this. He enjoys doing this work, and many times he has felt his ancestors' presence with him as he was performing these ordinances for them. He tells Sarah about his experiences, and she is very pleased to hear of his excitement in doing this, and of the impressions he feels there.

Some time later, Randy receives authorization from the Church that he can now go and perform all the necessary ordinance work for his own brother, Dean, at the temple. He is extremely excited to do this for him. He first goes to the baptistry and is baptized and confirmed for him. When he does this, he strongly feels Dean's presence with him, and feels that Dean is very joyful and is accepting these ordinances for himself. After this is finished, he goes up to the other areas to perform his other needed ordinances. When Randy is finishing the last part of these, he feels Dean's presence so strongly that he becomes very emotional. He could feel that Dean is almost giving him a hug, expressing his extreme gratitude and love to him for doing this important ordinance work for him.

That evening, he calls Sarah to tell her about the experience he had that day. He says on the phone, "Sarah, you won't believe what happened today. I had the most wonderful experience in the temple. Today, I completed all the ordinance work for my brother, Dean. Sarah, I could actually feel him there, showing his great love to me for doing this for him. It was such a wonderful, special feeling. Now I really know that people can continue to progress, and that they can receive more blessings. I know the Lord's plan for families and for their progression."

"Oh, Randy, this is so wonderful to hear. I'm so happy for you. You are experiencing for yourself how our Savior loves us and helps us, and how we can feel His joy in our lives. It's great that Dean is accepting these important ordinances, and that he is continuing to progress toward our Savior."

They talk a while longer about the importance of this work, and about his growth and development as he is more firmly dedicated to progress toward the Lord and receive His many blessings He has for each of us.

Randy continues going to the temple each week, to do ordinance work for his ancestors. Many times, these temple visits are coordinated with Sarah and Wayne, and at times with Ethan and Ruth, so they can all be there together. Quite often they have some great experiences as they are performing this work for their ancestors.

A few months later, Randy stops by Wayne and Sarah's home for a surprise visit on a Sunday afternoon. Sarah opens the door, and is very surprised to see a lovely woman standing next to him. She invites them in and asks, "Randy, who is this beautiful girl you brought with you?"

He replies, "I'm very excited to have you meet my fiancée, Melanie." Sarah shakes hands with her. "I met her at the temple. After I finished the session there, I felt like I needed to stay in the foyer area for a while, and ponder what I was feeling, enjoying the Spirit in the House of the Lord."

Melanie adds, "And that's when I came into his life. I wasn't sure if I should really go there that day, but then I had this strong feeling that I should go there right at that moment. I traveled there as soon as I could, wondering why I was having such a strong impression to go right then. I went inside and noticed Randy sitting there by himself. I felt that I should introduce myself to him, and now I'm part of his life." She smiles happily.

Sarah invites them to have a seat in the living room. While doing this, she joyfully says, "I'm so happy to meet you, Melanie."

After taking their seats, Randy continues, "You see, after she introduced herself to me, I invited her to sit down and we started talking. I told her about my recent experiences, and about how I have been feeling the Lord's Spirit much more in my life now. I explained how I had been praying about having a forever family. Melanie then said that she received this strong feeling to go there, and we both felt that it was so she could meet me."

"That's right. As we were talking, I felt this strong need to tell him about my life situation. I told him that my husband left me some time ago, and that I have an adult son and daughter. I explained that I am living on my own, and that I now feel that I need to be married in the temple this time to a wonderful husband. I have been praying about this, and I know the Lord answered my prayer when I met Randy."

"I felt this, too, when we went to have lunch together. We talked some more, and we both felt a closer bond to each other. We individually prayed about our new relationship that night, and the next morning I called her on the phone, and we shared our overwhelming confirmations we felt about getting married. I explained that our Savior has a plan for us to be an eternal family together. Now we both feel so joyful. The following week, I proposed and Melanie accepted. We decided to surprise you with this wonderful news today."

"Well, I certainly am surprised," Sarah excitedly responds. "You both look so happy. I'm very excited for both of you!"

Just then, Wayne comes in, after having taken a short nap. He says, "I thought I heard people talking in here."

Sarah greets him and tells him, "Guess what? Randy brought his fiancée for us to meet. Her name is Melanie," Sarah says as she introduces her to Wayne.

"Happy to meet you," he says, as he shakes hands with her and then with Randy. He sits down next to Sarah.

Sarah then asks, "Have you both planned on a wedding date yet?"

"Yes," Randy joyfully responds. "It will be in four weeks, on Saturday at ten in the morning at the temple. We're so excited, and everyone's invited." Randy smiles at Melanie as they are holding hands.

"Oh, that sounds wonderful," responds Sarah. "I'll be sure to let everybody know, and I'm sure they'll be very excited, hearing this great news. I know they'll all want to be there."

"This will be a great time, and Melanie's son and daughter are coming as well. We will have a beautiful reception afterward, at her stake center."

"It sounds like you have everything well planned. Well, it sounds great, and we will look forward to being there."

They talk some more, then Randy announces that they need to go visit her son and daughter before it gets too late. They leave as Wayne and Sarah wish them well. Sarah then says to Wayne, "Isn't it wonderful that Randy is now following our Savior, and is being married in the temple? He is certainly on his way to being part of a forever family."

"It is wonderful," responds Wayne. "I'm happy for both of

them. It will be great to see him married in the temple. This will be a fun time for them."

The wedding day comes, and everyone's excited to be there and witness their special marriage. Alexis and Owen are also there, and congratulate them afterward, along with everybody else. Randy and Melanie have a photographer there to take some beautiful pictures of them after they are outside. Some wonderful group pictures are taken as well. Alexis then extends the invitation for everyone to enjoy lunch at their restaurant, as a gift to them. She is very excited to see her birth father progress to this point, and to see him now married in the temple. She sees her prayers for him have literally been answered.

As newlyweds, they accept the invitation, and Randy excitedly tells his wife, "Wait till you taste Lexi's cooking. I'm not just saying that because Lexi's my birth daughter. She has really excelled in culinary arts, and she's a professional chef."

"I am excited to taste her food at her restaurant," responds Melanie. "It's good that your birth son is here also, along with your former wife. I don't mind, because we are all family in our Savior's plan. It's great that we are all friends, and I'm looking forward to enjoying our lunch together."

They arrive at the restaurant, and Melanie is already impressed with the beautiful entrance and the large sign out front. She especially likes the decorations inside. The front attendant warmly greets them, and welcomes Alexis and Owen as they are returning there.

Alexis tells them, while looking at Melanie, "I'll personally prepare all your meals when your orders come in. Melanie, I know you'll love it."

She responds, "Thank you, Lexi. I'm sure I will."

Alexis leaves with Owen to go to the employee area. The attendant leads the others to a larger table in a comfortable location. Their server then comes and takes their orders in a very polite manner. Melanie is very impressed with the relaxing background music, and the kindness of the workers there.

Their food arrives, and Randy watches his new wife as everyone begins eating. After a few seconds, she shows a very surprised, excited look. She exclaims, "This is so, so good!"

He responds, "I knew you would like it. What do you think of Lexi now?"

"How on earth does she make this taste so good? I've never had anything like this before. She is definitely one of a kind."

"I'm not sure how she does it. She just has a great talent in preparing food."

Everyone enjoys this time together, enjoying the food and conversation. Melanie's son and daughter are also very impressed with the food, and are happy while getting to know everybody there. Randy and Melanie then tell the others that they need to leave very soon, as they have much to do before their reception. Her son and daughter will be helping them. Randy and his wife tell Sarah and family that they'll see them in the evening.

That evening, Sarah, Wayne, Ethan, and Ruth arrive at the reception honoring Randy and Melanie. Later, Alexis and Owen arrive and congratulate them again. Melanie expresses her great appreciation to Alexis for such a wonderful lunch. Randy then thanks her, along with Melanie's children. Everyone at the reception is very joyful that Randy and Melanie are beginning their new life together; everyone sees that they are happy as they are living according to the Lord's will, and as they are truly desiring to be a forever family with great love among all the family members.

Even though Ethan, Alexis, and Trisha are not part of Randy's family now, they are sealed as a forever, eternal family with their mother, Sarah, and their new father, Wayne. Their joy will continue to increase within their family bonds. Each of their families will begin and grow later, as is the case with Alexis and Owen, and their children already. As Owen and Alexis are married in the temple, they are beginning the process of being a forever family with their strong family bonds, which will be continuing after their lives on Earth are finished. The same is true with Randy and Melanie, and her two children who were sealed to them. Everyone knows that this is the Lord's will and plan for everyone.

Now to mention about Sarah's three children being sealed to her and to Wayne, as an eternal family. When Sarah and Wayne were married in the temple, Ethan and Alexis were there to be sealed to their parents, as a forever family. However, Sarah decided to wait to have Trisha sealed to them by proxy, as Alexis hadn't received her own temple ordinances yet. Sarah had the impression that she should wait until she felt that it was the right time.

One very special occasion to relate now is this: Contained in the prequel book to this work, titled *Living a Miracle*, is the full story of Trisha's life on the Earth. She had departed this life as a preteen, due to complications from a major brain tumor. She was extremely full of Christlike love, always showing love and gratitude, and always smiling. Ruth had a wonderful experience taking care of her during her last two months of life on Earth. This was a time which Ruth has always treasured, as those memories are very dear to her heart.

After Ruth received her own ordinances at the temple, Sarah felt the very strong impression to invite her to be proxy for Trisha's receiving her own ordinances, then for her sealing to Wayne and Sarah. Ruth felt extremely honored at this invitation. She emotionally expressed her gratitude to Sarah, and personally felt this was right for her to do.

On that day, the time comes for Ruth to be proxy for Trisha to receive her first ordinance, then her other main one in the instruction room. Ruth tells Sarah how she definitely feels that Trisha is right there during this time. As the main ordinance is concluding, Ruth feels overcome with much emotion. Ruth again tells Sarah and Wayne that she feels Trisha there with them. They feel this also. Ethan and Alexis are in attendance with them, and experience Trisha's presence with great emotion. They then go upstairs for this special sealing to parents to occur. They are in a beautiful room in the temple, and Ruth is called up to be proxy for Trisha's sealing to parents. She goes over to Wayne and Sarah at the altar, and they put their hands together. The sealing ordinance is then pronounced. When the spoken words of the ordinance are concluded, Ruth suddenly lowers her head and begins crying with joy. They all pause during this time, until she looks up again.

Sarah tenderly asks, "You feel Trish is right here with us, don't you?"

She responds very emotionally, saying, "She's actually here with me, hugging me, and expressing her great love and gratitude. She's telling me how extremely joyful she is that she's now sealed to you and to Wayne forever." Ruth sobs some more.

"What a precious, tender moment this is for you and for us," Sarah emotionally says. "I also feel her presence here, and she's hugging us. You really are part of our being an eternal family, and you will always have this sweet, eternal relationship with us."

They emotionally conclude this sealing session, and Sarah and Wayne talk with Ruth some more about this precious experience they just had together. Ethan and Alexis also express their emotions with them. They know how important and how real these ordinances actually are. They know that family members in the Spirit World who have passed on, are really right here, showing us a great amount of love.

Our Savior's invitation for all of us to become forever families is open to everybody, regardless of their present situation. Those who are not members of the Church will have this opportunity when they join our Savior's Church. Those who die before receiving these sealing ordinances in the temple to become forever families, will receive these by proxy for them. After receiving these ordinances, your forever family will be made sure by individually following Christ, by sincerely praying, by increasing your faith and trust in Christ and His plan for you, and by doing your very best in keeping His commandments.

By loving to become more like Christ by doing these things the best we are able, and by developing more Christlike love within ourselves as we associate with and serve others, we will joyfully receive all the tremendous blessings He has for us, individually and as sealed families forever, which will be beyond our comprehension. Our loving family bonds and emotional connections we presently experience with each member of our families will be increased hundreds of times as we continue on our path to be forever families, after this life is concluded. These promises are true as you proceed on the road to your forever family.

Epilogue

T HE stories within this book have shown us the real purpose of our lives here on Earth. They show the extreme importance of following Christ during our existence on this Earth, while not seeing Him. This is part of His divine plan for us. By divine design, we are born into physical bodies here, through our parents, as we made the choice in our pre-existence to do this. Each of us is even born into a certain family, according to Christ's perfect plan.

We are born into families here for a specific reason. This is only the beginning of our lives in family relationships, which are intended to continue and increase forever. This is our Savior's plan for us as families. However, on the other side of all this, Satan does not want any of this to occur. He wants to stop this beginning of family progression in any way he can. As part of God's plan, Christ is allowing Satan to tempt us and deceive us in many ways, without our being able to see him or Christ or our Heavenly Father. This is so we can show both of Them that we will choose, using our own free will, to follow Christ's words, no matter what.

As none of us is perfect in following Christ, He has lovingly provided His atoning sacrifice for us, satisfying the demands of our imperfections, so that we can ultimately receive His greatest reward in love, by doing the best we can to follow Him. We are taught that everyone in the Church who is on the straight and narrow covenant path that leads to Christ and His loving blessings, who is striving and struggling and desiring to do what is right, though is far from perfect in this life; if he passes out of this life while he's on the covenant path, he's going to go on to eternal reward in his Father's kingdom.

Christ loves each of us with all His heart. He knows the good and bad of our lives, our grief, our disappointments, our unrewarded efforts, our frustrations, and our temptations. He has shared His love with us, and He wants us to show our love by helping others. He asks us to repent of our shortcomings and our wrongdoings, and to be humble. He wants us to continually strive to improve, and to be full of hope and develop more faith and trust in Him. He desires that we proceed to do His work of gathering Israel and bringing other people to Him. This is part of the mission Christ gave us before we were born, along with following Him and becoming Christlike families. The best part is that He can greatly help us as we do this.

The important thing to remember as we strive to do what Christ wants us to do, is that Satan is working his hardest to deceive everyone. Satan *is* very real, and his forces are working very hard with him. The coming of Christ is nearing, and Satan knows he doesn't have much time left to accomplish his desires, that of stopping family progress in its tracks, and stopping people from completing their missions here. There are many, many deceptions coming from Satan now, as he is working harder than he ever has before, to prevent forever families. He is confusing many people so they don't understand God's law for families and family relationships; he is destroying families through his great tool of illegal drugs and substance abuse, and he is teaching people to learn how to hate and kill. He wants to destroy as many of us as possible, by working through as many people as he and his forces can, but the good thing to know is that he doesn't have the power to do so, as we stay strong with Christ and follow Him. When Christ comes again, Satan will lose to Christ, and he and his forces will be bound.

We are seeing more evidence of Satan's work in our world now, as his time is running short. This is all known to the Lord's prophets, and we know that calamities and destruction, along with even more of Satan's evil work will be increasing in the years ahead. We just need to step back, take a break for a moment, and observe and realize the reality of world conditions, and what they mean to us in the Lord's plan. Christ knows all the evil which will be occurring before His coming, and He has told us through His prophets how we can protect ourselves from evil, and receive the protection Christ has for us. In the coming days, we are told that it will not be possible for us to spiritually survive without the guiding, comforting, and spiritual influence of the Spirit of the Lord in our lives every day. As we pray about our concerns, our fears, and the very longings of our hearts, we will receive the promptings of what we need to do. God loves us and does want to speak to us and guide us. We can trust Him and find peace in Him, and know He is the real source of what is actually true.

As we do this and are obedient, we will receive guidance that will bring us joy during these turbulent times. As we are truly grateful for the blessings we receive from Him, and as we are patient while being obedient, we will receive answers, blessings, and even miracles. We *can* protect ourselves and our families from the impending evil which will be increasing and coming more forcefully. It is extremely important to follow Christ during these days of evil, as choosing to do this or not to do this will determine the outcome of our lives forever.

We should remember that everything is known to our Savior, and He has His perfect plan for each one of us. When people develop lifelong diseases, have debilitating accidents, or die or are killed early in life, we can know that these are not just chance happenings, or occurrences of bad luck. These are all part of the Lord's plan, for His specific reasons which we may not fully understand at the time. Those who are doing what's right and are victims of evil designs, will receive their blessed rewards from Christ. Someone who is killed, even intentionally, is not dying before his time, as everything concerning Heavenly Father's children is known to Him and to Christ, and He has His perfect plan for this person in the Spirit World, already knowing the time he will be entering there.

Our Savior knows our lives to the smallest detail, and He will lovingly assist us through means of His grace, in the greatest manner possible, as we let Him. He can strengthen us and help us through coming tumultuous times, as He greatly desires our salvation, as well as our receiving tremendous blessings, as our families continue eternally. So, what are some of these blessings? We can receive crowning glories, and become all-knowing and eternally loving with incomprehensible love as Christ now has, basically becoming as He is. We can receive eternal increase in posterity, and reign over them in great love, helping them to increase their love, and to grow and progress toward receiving tremendous blessings as well. As they do this, they will continue blessing our lives through the eternities. However, all of this is accomplished only as an eternal family unit, not as individuals. Our own families will also continue to increase.

For those who are not able to have families in this life, such as is the case with Ruth in this story, our Savior will allow these righteous people to begin their own families during the millennium, our existence after Christ comes, where He will reign personally on the Earth. Everyone will receive a resurrected body during this time, which will be physically perfect, where there will be no pain, disease, or death. The amount of glory our resurrected bodies will receive depends on our faithfulness here, our real intent of heart in following Christ.

Our Savior has a perfect, glorious plan which follows His perfect order for the faithful, and for the innocent, for those righteous spirits whose bodies die before the age of accountability, and those whose bodies are not able to physically develop to allow the person to be accountable on this Earth. This is also part of His plan for these people and their families, which He planned for them before their births. Children who die will be raised from the age of their deaths in perfect bodies, after Christ's coming.

Here's a little more information now, concerning forever families. Our Savior will make sure that eternal family relationships are fair and good for all who are faithful. Each faithful person will receive *all* the blessings our Lord has for us, no matter the choices of other family members. He will fulfill your desire for the blessing of an eternal family as you keep your covenants and follow Him, and as you help your family do the same, as guided by the Spirit of the Lord. Sealed spouses who maintain complete fidelity and follow the Lord will treasure their relationship, which begins their eternal family, and will continue to increase after this life.

By knowing more about our Savior's real plan for us and the joyful blessings He has reserved for us, it would be very sensible to follow His words which include His gospel teachings, to receive the necessary ordinances He provides for us, and to make sacred covenants with Him in the temple, in His house, so that we can be sealed by His authority, within His law, and become forever families with even greater love and eternal increase, as He has lovingly intended for us.

Now, to conclude the story presented in this sequel. About three years later, Ruth Shepherd was attending a stake fireside meeting, where she met a very wonderful, tender, spiritual member of the Church who had never been married and had not yet met the right person who he felt was to be his wife. He is of her same race, and she felt a special closeness to him as he was getting to know her. They became engaged and were later married in the temple, where everyone attended.

Sarah, her family, the Hopkinson family, and Randy and Melanie Wilkinson all attended the wedding and are now very excited for her, knowing that she won't be alone, and that she is actually beginning the process to have her very own forever family. Ruth is so extremely joyful with this blessed event in her life. She thanks Heavenly Father and Jesus Christ in prayer every day for Their loving kindness They have shown her, as she has been striving to be obedient to Christ's perfect gospel plan. She knows that she will begin having her own children during the millennium, who are waiting for her, which makes her very, very happy.

Everyone is doing quite well during these ensuing years. Alexis Hopkinson is very successful with her restaurant and is thoroughly enjoying it. She has received her Master of Arts degree and is now internationally recognized and renowned as a professional, certified grand master chef, with several awards and accreditations to her name. She frequently travels abroad to meet with other international master chefs who desire to bring her patented, trademarked recipes and procedures for the preparation of her exquisite entrées and dishes into their respective countries, on a contractual basis. However, she plans to always be home on Sunday with her family to attend her church meetings, as she knows this is extremely important. Alexis has been called to be the Primary president in her ward.

Alexis and Owen have a third child, a tender, happy boy named Tyler, who is now a few years old. Their two girls are growing up very well. Christine is an extremely loving, spiritual girl, who has been attending school and is accomplishing more there than was first thought she could. She frequently smiles and converses in a sweet, loving manner. Many members in her Church ward enjoy seeing and being around her as they feel her spirituality, and she is a favorite in her Primary class. Owen and Alexis are always showing gratitude to the

Lord for their sweet children and their many blessings as they continue to follow our Savior. (They are all depicted on the cover of this book.)

Sarah Spencer has retired from her profession, and Ethan Wilkinson is now the company supervisor and manager in the consultation building there. Sarah and Wayne travel, at times, to visit historical sites, including historic Church sites. One time, they take Ethan with them to go visit Robert, and catch him up with all the happenings in the family. He is very happy to hear how the Lord has blessed everybody. Later, Ethan mentions that he has a girlfriend who is seriously interested in him. He announces that a proposal could be coming soon. This makes Sarah and everyone especially joyful.

So continues our quest to become forever families. In this trilogy, we have seen how our Savior's hand is greatly involved in our lives, as we let Him help us in our daily living. As all that has been explained here about our future existence after Christ's coming is very true and real, as has been revealed to us by His prophets, many people here, and those in the Spirit World know what marvelous blessings await them as they are faithful and do their best to follow Christ. These people are experiencing more happiness in their lives as they do this, and as they receive their essential ordinances in His house, including the all-important sealing ordinance. May you be inspired to do the same, to be sealed as a family in the Lord's house when you are ready, and to diligently follow Christ, so that your loving families may continue on with tremendous love and blessings, forever.

HAVING read this beautiful story concerning our Savior's loving plan for us and our families, many of you may have encountered some new perspectives, beyond what was already brought to light in my prequel, *Living a Miracle.* Depending on your present situation in life, along with your family's situation, and your depth of knowledge of and progression toward Christ on your path toward Him, perhaps some of you might think that part of this information may be fantasy, even though you presently experience very strong, loving, emotional connections with your other family members, which run deep. There are those of you who are already closer to Christ, who greatly comprehend His tremendous, majestic love for you, and who know and can feel of the verity and certainty of His crowning blessings for us as we strive to follow Him and become more like Him.

As you ponder the story related here, and the stories in my other books, you most likely have been able to intensely identify with at least one of the particular characters. By doing this, you can see how the Lord's hand has been in your life more than you were previously aware. You may have even felt a special feeling, indicating to you that this information concerning the Spirit World and our continuation of life with greater blessings is actually true. I can tell you that I know it is, through my studies of the completeness of Christ's gospel which has been revealed up to this time, and through the feelings He has given me, allowing me a true understanding of our purpose here in life with our trials, along with a more complete understanding of Christ's all-encompassing, eternal atoning sacrifice, which makes all His powerful blessings possible and available to everyone.

Jesus Christ was born on this Earth and He willingly accomplished His sacred mission here, as a result of His true, incomprehensible love for us, that only He could do as part of His great calling from our Heavenly Father, so that we have the opportunity to literally become glorified beings as He is, and receive all the blessings He presently experiences, including the continuation of our families in great glory. This *is* His plan for us.

Here are a few questions to ponder as you read and re-read the stories presented in my books. By doing this, you will receive more thoughts and impressions individually, and as a family or as a group, as you incorporate these books into a book club reading.

1. How has our Savior, Jesus Christ blessed you, especially during severe trials? How do you feel His loving assistance and comfort increase as you pray for help, and as you frequently remember Him and put Him more into your daily life?

2. How has your family blessed your life? What joyful memories have you had with your family? How has a particular family member helped you, whether in your family growing up, or with your own family you've had?

3. How have friends or acquaintances helped you during a time of need, after having prayed about it? Have you thought that these people were guided through the Lord's Spirit to help you, as an answer to your prayer?

4. Why are some people born with lifelong disabilities or disorders? Why do some develop major health issues or are involved in major, life-changing accidents?

5. What are your thoughts concerning the Spirit World? What do you think about those people who have had an out-of-the-body experience, then returned to tell about it?

6. What are your opinions about why we have such strong, loving family connections? Do you really think Christ planned this and wants this to continue forever?

7. Why are some people not given the opportunity to have their own children in this life? How will the Lord bless them now, such as through adoption, as well as after this life is over? Do you believe that adoption of children is part of our Savior's perfect plan? Are you aware that these adopted children can be sealed to their parents forever, within the everlasting covenant of marriage according to God's law? Share your thoughts about these people being able to have their own children after this life. Will our own families continue to increase after Christ's coming?

8. What are your thoughts concerning Christ's atonement? What other areas of your life does His atoning sacrifice cover, besides forgiving us of our repentant sins?

9. What are your true thoughts about the title of this book? Why do you want your loving family connections you now experience, to continue forever?

10. How do other families help us? How do we help them? How have you felt the Lord's Spirit in your life, as you help and serve others?

11. How does this story help you increase your good perspective of yourself, as you think of how it reflects on your own life? What do you think is your mission in life? Where do you think you will be in life ten years from now? Do you think you'll be closer to accomplishing the mission and calling Christ gave you to accomplish here? Do you think you'll be more Christlike? This would be something very important to consider as Christ's coming is drawing closer. In line with this, why are we not told the exact timing of Christ's coming?

12. How is Christ able to give you comfort as world conditions continue to worsen? Do you really believe that He knows everything about you, and knows the best way to help you, no matter what happens in your life?

13. Why is it more important now to resist Satan and follow Christ? Why is it important to develop more faith and trust in Him and His plan for you? Do you believe that good music can help you and inspire you in your life, as you strive to follow Christ?

14. Do you really believe that by following Christ, you can be truly happier now and receive nonstop, incomprehensible blessings after this life?

15. For those of you who have read all three books in this series, what have been your personal experiences as you have followed the experiences and emotions of the many characters throughout these stories? As you talk about these characters' feelings as a group, such as in a book club, what insights have you gained about each of your missions on Earth? How has it been an enjoyable, profitable time for you?

I, Robert Callaway, truly hope that this reading guide has inspired all of you to take an inventory of your lives, and to feel the urgent need to dedicate yourselves to Christ by re-membering Him, learning of Him, and following Him, doing what He has taught us to do. By doing these simple things, and by helping others and by constantly spreading joy, hope, kindness, love, and peace through our good actions and exam-ples, we will be drawing ourselves closer to Him. It is simply a matter of focusing our true intent of heart to following Christ. This is so extremely important to do now, the best we are able, as this will determine the type of lives we will have forever. This applies to all of us, no matter what walk of life we're in, as Christ's atonement applies to every person, and each of us *will* have the wonderful opportunity to receive His greatest blessings, which includes eternal families.

— Robert Callaway

Afterword

Our loving Savior will definitely help us to become forever families as we sincerely strive to follow Him. You have read about the great blessings our Savior has for us, including true happiness, as we work on developing our talents, as we prepare ourselves to be guided by His Spirit, as we truly serve others, and as we positively endure our trials and accept the wonderful, kind assistance which Christ especially desires to give us throughout our lives here on Earth. You have seen the reality of how our families will actually be able to continue together forever with increasing blessings, beyond those blessings we receive in this life.

We are all able to receive greater happiness and more blessings, no matter our present situation. Through prayer and following Christ more in our lives, we will receive help and even miracles as blessings for us, as shown in this story. Through the experiences of the characters in all three books, you have seen how Jesus Christ has been the central theme throughout, and has been the means of blessing people. Many times He works through other people to accomplish His plans for them. We can make it through life with Christ's help, no matter what situation we're in and what trials we are given according to His plan. We are then able to literally become the same as Christ and our Heavenly Father and Heavenly Mother are now, with eternal increase. This is the purpose of our existence in this life, and the purpose of our families.

Our Heavenly Father and His Son, Jesus Christ are definitely real, are glorified living people, and have a glorious plan with many blessings in reserve for everyone who has ever lived on this Earth. The realization of these great blessings depends on our true intent of heart, and the choices we make through our agency, a gift given to us by Christ. As we turn our true intent of heart to following Christ and becoming like Him, we will continually feel pure love, and we will receive great happiness and true joy with all our families throughout the eternities.

About Atmosphere Press

Atmosphere Press is an independent, full-service publisher for excellent books in all genres and for all audiences. Learn more about what we do at atmospherepress.com.

We encourage you to check out some of Atmosphere's latest releases, which are available at Amazon.com and via order from your local bookstore:

Icarus Never Flew 'Round Here, by Matt Edwards

COMFREY, WYOMING: Maiden Voyage, by Daphne Birkmeyer

The Chimera Wolf, by P.A. Power

Umbilical, by Jane Kay

The Two-Blood Lion, by Nick Westfield

Shogun of the Heavens: The Fall of Immortals, by I.D.G. Curry

Hot Air Rising, by Matthew Taylor

30 Summers, by A.S. Randall

Delilah Recovered, by Amelia Estelle Dellos

A Prophecy in Ash, by Julie Zantopoulos

The Killer Half, by JB Blake

Ocean Lessons, by Karen Lethlean

Unrealized Fantasies, by Marilyn Whitehorse

The Mayari Chronicles: Initium, by Karen McClain

Squeeze Plays, by Jeffrey Marshall

JADA: Just Another Dead Animal, by James Morris

Hart Street and Main: Metamorphosis, by Tabitha Sprunger

Karma One, by Colleen Hollis

Ndalla's World, by Beth Franz

Adonai, by Arman Isayan

About the Author

ROBERT CALLAWAY was born in Hollywood, California, and moved with his parents and sister to Utah when he was six. He grew up in the Orem-Provo area.

He attended BYU for two and a half years, where he studied science, mathematics, and education. He also studied medical transcription and office management.

Robert was employed in building maintenance, and has been self-employed in the food industry with his wife.

All his life, he has enjoyed learning about and observing the weather.

Robert was diagnosed with Asperger's Syndrome at age 36. He has overcome practically all of this disorder and presently lives in a small town in Utah.